THE JESUS I NEVER KNEW

Leader's Guide

PHILIP YANCEY
written by Sheryl Moon

ZONDERVAN

GRAND RAPIDS, MICHIGAN 49530 US

ZONDERVAN™

The Jesus I Never Knew Leader's Guide
Copyright © 1998 by Philip D. Yancey

Requests for information should be addressed to:

ZondervanPublishingHouse
Grand Rapids, Michigan 49530

ISBN: 0-310-22432-2

Interior art by Florence Chambers
Interior design by Sue Vandenberg Koppenol

Some editorial material adapted from *The Jesus I Never Knew Study Guide* by Philip Yancey with Brenda Quinn.

Printed in the United States of America

06 /❖ VG/ 17 16 15 14 13 12 11

THE JESUS I NEVER KNEW

Leader's Guide

Resources by Philip Yancey

The Jesus I Never Knew
What's So Amazing About Grace?
The Bible Jesus Read
Reaching for the Invisible God
Where Is God When It Hurts?
Disappointment with God
The Student Bible, General Edition (with Tim Stafford)
Meet the Bible (with Brenda Quinn)
Church: Why Bother?
Finding God in Unexpected Places
I Was Just Wondering
Soul Survivor

Books by Philip Yancey and Dr. Paul Brand

Fearfully and Wonderfully Made
In His Image
The Gift of Pain

Contents

Introduction

Foreword

Philip Yancey's study of Jesus began with a class he taught at LaSalle Street Church in Chicago. The use of movies about the life of Jesus, the discussion from class members, and his personal study all combined to give him a new view of Jesus—hence the title of his book *The Jesus I Never Knew.*

Yet all along he had another goal in mind: He wanted his quest for Jesus to serve as a guide for other people. As Yancey himself wrote, "In the end, what does it matter if a reader learns about 'The Jesus Philip Yancey Never Knew?' What matters infinitely more is for *you* to get to know Jesus."

For this reason, we have produced a curriculum to help you delve into the topic with a class of your own using movies as a springboard for discussion. Finding the right video clips and obtaining permission to show them can be a long and tedious task—this curriculum takes that step away from you! Philip Yancey recommended the best clips for each topic and we obtained permission to include them in this curriculum. For each session we have provided several different film clips along with a brief teaching segment with Philip Yancey and a variety of exercises and discussion questions to help the participants of your class begin to think about the Jesus *they* never knew.

This course is bound to change the perceptions of those who seriously engage themselves in it. With a willingness to tackle difficult questions, Philip Yancey helps us to look at the radical words of Jesus and ask whether we are taking him seriously enough in our own day and age. For those who have been raised in the church and have known Jesus all of their lives, *and* for those who are meeting Jesus for the first time, Philip Yancey challenges us to think about this man as the Bible presents him—brilliant, creative, challenging, fearless, compassionate, unpredictable, and ultimately satisfying. You will find that the video clips combined with Bible study and your own discussion will help you to discover the Jesus *you* never knew!

This Kit Contains

- *The Jesus I Never Knew*—This is the award-winning book by Philip Yancey in which he offers his perspective on the life of Christ and his work—his teaching, his miracles, his death and resurrection—and ultimately, who he was and why he came. This book is based on Yancey's own discoveries as he led a group in Chicago through a similar approach to taking a look at Jesus.

- *The Jesus I Never Knew Video*—A fourteen-part video series of live sessions with Philip Yancey as well as different film clips portraying the life of Jesus. These ten-minute video vignettes will serve as the basis for your discussion in each session.

- *The Jesus I Never Knew Leader's Guide*—This comprehensive guide provides all the information you will need to lead your group through the different sessions of this course.

- *The Jesus I Never Knew Participant's Guide*—This workbook contains questions and exercises for each session, designed to help participants process the material.

Additional kits and copies of the Participant's Guide as well as the book are available from:

Zondervan Publishing House
5300 Patterson Avenue SE
Grand Rapids, MI 49530
Phone: 1–800–727–3480

How This Leader's Guide Is Organized

This Leader's Guide is divided into fourteen sessions. Each 45-minute session corresponds to a chapter in Philip Yancey's book *The Jesus I Never Knew*.

For each session *the leader* will need:

Leader's Guide
Bible
Philip Yancey's Book *The Jesus I Never Knew*
Video Player, Monitor, Stand, Extension Cord, etc.
Videotape

For each session *each participant* will need:

Participant's Guide
Bible
Pen or Pencil
Philip Yancey's Book *The Jesus I Never Knew* (optional)

Each session is divided into five parts: Before You Lead, Introduction, Warm-Up, Content, and Summary.

1. Before You Lead

Synopsis

This material is provided for the leader's information. It is a summary of the ideas contained in Philip Yancey's book and presents the main ideas for the session.

Session Outline

An overview of the content and activities to be covered throughout the session.

Materials

The materials listed above are critical for both the leader and each participant. In this section you will find a list of *additional* materials needed for this specific session. Additional materials are needed in sessions 1, 2, and 11.

Recommended Reading

The leader is encouraged to read the appropriate chapter of Philip Yancey's book *The Jesus I Never Knew* in preparation for each session.

2. Introduction

Includes calling the class together, an opening prayer, and a brief review.

3. Warm-Up

These exercises and/or questions are designed to help everyone begin thinking about the session topic. A corresponding page is found in the Participant's Guide.

4. Content

The bulk of the session is focused on content that you will walk through. The session material is found on the left-hand page of the Leader's Guide. You may want to read the material word for word, or you might just want to highlight key words and phrases. We encourage you to amplify various points with your own material illustrations. Make it personal!

On the right-hand page is a copy of the corresponding Participant's Guide page(s). There is also space on this right-hand page for the leader to write in any additional planning notes. Having the corresponding Participant's Guide page in front of you allows you to view the page the participants are seeing as you talk without having to hold two books at the same time. It also lets you know where the participants are in their book when someone asks you a question.

The Content section also includes the following key typographical elements:

1. Statements the instructor should read verbatim are set off with a special bullet. ❖ These statements correlate to statements also included in the Participant's Guide. Words shown in ALL CAPITAL LETTERS are words the participants need to fill in the blanks found on the corresponding pages in their Participant's Guides:

Example:

❖ ONE-THIRD of all people on earth claim to be Christians.

2. Directions to the instructor are enclosed in a shaded box and are not meant to be spoken:

> Solicit responses from the group.

3. The instructor narrative is shown in standard typeface.

Video Vignette

Each of the sessions has a corresponding video clip including a short teaching segment by Philip Yancey and appropriate film clips related to the topic. The content of each vignette is shown in italics for the leader's information and there is a corresponding page in the Participant's Guide for notes. The video portion of the session will provide a springboard for class discussion.

Exercises

These will be done either alone, in small groups, or with the group as a whole. Directions are included for each exercise. This material is also included in the Participant's Guide.

Depending on your particular setting you can lengthen or shorten each session to accommodate your specific situation. Be aware that discussion times may run longer or shorter than you plan. Try to have an "alternate" plan for each session—know where you can cut time or add an additional discussion question or two if you need to.

5. Summary

This section will include a review of what was covered in the session as well as a suggestion for additional reading in *The Jesus I Never Knew*.

6. Appendix

In the appendix, you will find a complete listing of all the sources for the video clips that have been included on the video tape.

If you wish to include additional video clips, we have also included a brief summary of other movies that may prove useful, along with Philip Yancey's own very subjective evaluation (his words). You'll see that we list some portions of the movies that may apply to each week's meeting. There is an approximate time frame for where in the movie each scene appears, but these are merely estimates; different editions of movies vary slightly in the timing of these scenes. When we say "forty-five-minute mark," you may find that the scene referred to appears at the forty- or fifty-minute mark in your version. You may have to scan forward or backward to find the precise place.

If you decide to utilize some of these additional clips, please heed the instructions regarding permissions.

Before the First Session

- Read the first chapter of *The Jesus I Never Knew* and go over the entire lesson plan for the first session as outlined in the Leader's Guide.

- Watch the video session material.

- Obtain the necessary Participant's Guides for all participants. Consider also having available for purchase copies of Philip Yancey's book *The Jesus I Never Knew*.

- Look ahead to session 2 and 11 for the additional materials you will need, to avoid having to scramble at the last minute.

Five Tips for Leading Group Discussion

1. Allow group members to participate at their own comfort level. Everyone need not answer every question.

2. Ask questions with interest and warmth and then listen carefully to individual responses. Remember: No answer is too insignificant. Encourage and affirm each person's participation.

3. Be flexible: Reword questions if necessary. Take the liberty of adding or deleting questions to accommodate the needs of your group members.

4. Allow for (and expect) differences of opinion and experience.

5. DO NOT BE AFRAID OF SILENCE! Allow people time to think—don't panic. Sometimes 10 seconds of silence seems like an eternity. Some of this material is difficult to process—allow people time to digest the question and *then* respond.

Session One:
The Jesus
I Thought I Knew

Before You Lead

Synopsis

I first got acquainted with Jesus when I was a child, singing "Jesus Loves Me" in Sunday school, addressing bedtime prayers to "Dear Lord Jesus," watching Bible club teachers move cutout figures across a flannel graph board. I associated Jesus with Kool-Aid and sugar cookies and gold stars for good attendance.

Later, while attending a Bible college, I encountered a different image. A painting popular in those days depicted Jesus, hands outstretched, suspended in a Dali-like pose over the United Nations building in New York City. In 1971 the film *The Gospel According to St. Matthew,* by Italian filmmaker Pier Paolo Pasolini, again helped to force a disturbing revaluation of my image of Jesus. In Pasolini's portrayal, in physical appearance Jesus favored those who would have been kicked out of Bible college and rejected by most churches. Among his contemporaries, the Bible says he somehow gained a reputation as a "winebibber and a glutton." Those in authority, whether religious or political, regarded him as a troublemaker, a disturber of the peace. He spoke and acted like a revolutionary, scorning fame, family, property, and other traditional measures of success.

I have studied Jesus extensively in Catholic, liberal Protestant, and conservative evangelical seminaries. For two years I taught a class on the life of Jesus, using a variety of movies about his life as a springboard for discussion. In all of my study, I learned that whenever I returned to the Gospels, the fog that accompanied an academic approach seemed to lift. The films about Jesus helped restore Jesus' humanity. Jesus, I found, was far less tame than the Jesus I had met in Sunday school and Bible college. He seemed more emotional than the average person is, not less. More passionate, not less. How is it then, that the church has tamed such a character?

In my book I attempt to tell the story of Jesus, not my own story. Inevitably, though, a search for Jesus turns out to be one's own search. No one who meets Jesus ever stays the same. I have found that the doubts that afflict me from many sources—from science, from comparative religion, from an innate defect of skepticism, from aversion to the church—take on a new light when I bring those doubts to the man named Jesus.

Session Outline

I. Introduction
   Welcome
   Prayer

II. Warm-Up
   The Twentieth-Century View of Jesus

III. Content
   Video Vignette
   Class Response
   Personal Reflection
   Facts About Jesus
   Bible Study

IV. Summary
   Review
   Suggested Reading for Participants

Materials

Whiteboard, newsprint, or overhead projector (with appropriate stands, cords, and pens) to be used for the warm-up.

Recommended Reading

"The Jesus I Thought I Knew," chapter 1 of *The Jesus I Never Knew*

Session One:
The Jesus I Thought I Knew

Introduction *(3 minutes)*

Welcome

> Call the group together.
> Welcome the participants to session 1 of *The Jesus I Never Knew* course: "The Jesus I Thought I Knew."
> Introduce yourself: Tell the group your name, a little about yourself and your family, and why you are excited about teaching this course.

Prayer

Heavenly Father, thank you for the opportunity you have given us to come together as we journey toward getting to know you in a new way. Guide our thoughts and our hearts as we seek to experience you like we never have before. In Jesus' name. Amen.

Warm-Up *(5–10 minutes)*

The Twentieth-Century View of Jesus

> Participant's Guide page 9

For fourteen sessions we are going to be studying the life of Jesus—for many of us, in a way we never have before! This course is based on Philip Yancey's best-selling book *The Jesus I Never Knew*.

> Hold book up. At this point you may wish to offer this book for sale as an additional resource or simply mention where a copy can be obtained.

Planning Notes

_____
_____
_____
_____
_____
_____
_____
_____
_____
_____
_____
_____
_____
_____
_____
_____
_____
_____
_____
_____
_____
_____
_____
_____
_____
_____
_____

Session One:
The Jesus I Thought I Knew

Questions To Consider

- How do I perceive Jesus?

- Who is Philip Yancey, and how can films help me to see Jesus in a new way?

- What is *my* answer to the question, "Who is this man, Jesus?"

9

Today we are going to be identifying our present perceptions of Jesus. We will also be introduced to Philip Yancey, who will ultimately confront us with the question, "Who is this man, Jesus?" In just a few minutes we'll be introduced to Yancey's use of films as he got to know Jesus in a new way, but for now let's focus on *our* perceptions of Jesus today.

Participant's Guide page 10

Turn to page 10 in your Participant's Guide. As we move along through this material, we'll be discussing various topics together as a large group and in small groups. We will also have some exercises to work on alone. The Participant's Guide will help us to stay focused and will provide the resources we need to see Jesus in a new way.

This first exercise is designed to help us identify the Jesus we know in the twentieth century.

Record the answers to the following questions on a whiteboard, newsprint, or overhead projector.

◆ What one word would a church member choose to describe Jesus?

Solicit responses from the group.
Possible Answers: Shepherd, Friend, Counselor, Provider, Savior, Lord, King of Kings, Son of God

---

◆ How would one of your neighbors or one of your coworkers describe Jesus?

Solicit responses from the group.
Possible Answers: Tyrant, hippie, radical, who?, philosopher, religious teacher, good man

---

◆ In your mind's eye, what did Jesus look like? Tall? Short? Handsome? Curly hair or straight? Did he have a dark or light complexion? Where did you get this picture of him (films, paintings, books, Sunday school)? Can you describe specific images from the past?

Solicit responses from the group.

Planning Notes

_____

_____

_____

_____

_____

_____

_____

_____

_____

_____

_____

_____

_____

_____

_____

_____

_____

_____

_____

_____

_____

_____

_____

_____

_____

_____

_____

_____

10   The Jesus I Never Knew Participant's Guide

The Twentieth-Century View of Jesus

What one word would a church member choose to describe Jesus?

How would one of your neighbors or one of your coworkers describe Jesus?

In your mind's eye, what did Jesus look like? Tall? Short? Handsome? Curly hair or straight? Did he have a dark or light complexion? Where did you get this picture of him (films, paintings, books, Sunday school)? Can you describe specific images from the past?

Content *(30–35 minutes)*

Video Vignette *(approximately 10 minutes)*

> Participant's Guide page 11

Philip Yancey's own journey is an interesting one as we consider the topic of "The Jesus I Thought I Knew." In this first video segment we will have the opportunity to meet Philip and be introduced to the concept of using films as a means to seeing Jesus in a new way. Following Philip Yancey's introduction, there will be three film clips. Use the space provided on page 11 of your Participant's Guide to record an adjective or impression that describes your reactions or feelings. If you need some help getting started, the questions are provided to guide you.

> View Video Vignette
>
> *Philip Yancey*—Personal introduction to the course, including the different images he had of Jesus and how and why movies can help us
>
> *King of Kings*—Jesus healing a child's doll
>
> *The Gospel According to St. Matthew*—Political-type Jesus teaching the disciples. This Italian movie has the spoken English dubbed in so the lip movements don't always perfectly match the words.
>
> *Son of Man*—Nontraditional Jesus in the temple. This clip presents a very unusual portrayal of Jesus by a British actor.

As you can see, he gives us a great deal to think about! Let's take a few minutes to discuss your impressions.

Class Response *(5–10 minutes)*

> Solicit responses from the group to the following questions.

1. Share the adjectives or first impressions you used to describe each film.

2. Which film most closely presented your idea of Jesus? Which film seemed to contrast your idea of Jesus?

Personal Reflection *(5 minutes)*

> Participant's Guide page 12

In the video vignette, Philip Yancey presented some of the different perceptions of Jesus he had at different times in his life. Turn to page 12 in your Guide. This exercise is designed to help you begin to think about the different stages in your life and how you related to and experienced Jesus at those times.

Planning Notes

_____

_____

_____

_____

_____

_____

_____

_____

_____

_____

_____

_____

_____

_____

_____

_____

_____

_____

_____

_____

_____

_____

_____

_____

_____

_____

_____

_____

_____

_____

_____

Video Notes
Philip Yancey

As you watch the following scenes from these three films, think of one adjective or impression that describes your reactions or feelings. If you need some help, use the questions below as a guide.

Kings of Kings

Is this like the image of Jesus you had growing up?

The Gospel According to St. Matthew

Do you find anything disturbing about Pasolini's Jesus?

Son of Man

Can you imagine Jesus being overweight?
Can you imagine Jesus ever saying, "Shut up!"?

Personal Reflection

In the first column the various stages of your life are listed for you. For each stage think of the major people and events that influenced you. Record your responses in column 2. In column 3 jot down how you related to or experienced Christ at that time.

Stage of Life	Major Influence	My Experience/ Thoughts/Relationship
Childhood		
Teen Years		
College Days		
Adult Life		

In the first column the various stages of your life are listed for you. For each stage think of the major people and events that influenced you. Record these in column 2. In column 3 you can jot down how you related to Christ in response to those major influences.

Any questions? We'll take about 5 minutes to work on this exercise.

> Allow participants 5 minutes to reflect. Let them know when they have 1 minute left.

Our time is up. Five minutes go by so quickly! Hopefully you're beginning to think about your perceptions of Jesus and how they influence your relationship with him.

Facts About Jesus (3 minutes)

> Participant's Guide page 13

Let's move on to page 13 in your Guide and take a look at the facts we have about Jesus at this point in history. There are several times throughout this course when you will have pages that look similar to this one. I'm going to give you the answers to the blank spaces—No, you don't have to guess!—and then I will give you some amplified information. Feel free to take whatever additional notes you find helpful.

❖ The birth of Jesus DIVIDED history.

No matter what people may believe about it, the birth of Jesus was so important that everything that has ever happened on this planet falls into a category of before Christ or after Christ.

❖ ONE-THIRD of all people on earth claim to be Christians.

❖ The name of Jesus has become COMMON, even used as a SWEAR WORD.

In the Western world, people use Jesus' name as an expletive. It's a strange relationship, but those who most often despise him use his name on a regular basis. We just cannot get away from this man Jesus.

❖ The perceptions we have of Jesus have been muddied by:

❖ TIME

Let's face it, this is the twentieth century. Two thousand years have passed since Jesus walked and talked on this earth. We cannot recapture what his time on earth was *really* like.

❖ SCHOLARSHIP

A scholar at the University of Chicago estimates that more has been written about Jesus in the last twenty years than in the previous nineteen centuries. There are currently over 65,000 books about Jesus in print. However, Jesus is portrayed in many different ways: as a political revolutionary, a magician,

Planning Notes

_____

_____

_____

_____

_____

_____

_____

_____

_____

_____

_____

_____

_____

_____

_____

_____

_____

_____

_____

_____

_____

_____

_____

_____

_____

_____

_____

_____

---

12   The Jesus I Never Knew Participant's Guide

Personal Reflection

In the first column the various stages of your life are listed for you. For each stage think of the major people and events that influenced you. Record your responses in column 2. In column 3 jot down how you related to or experienced Christ at that time.

Stage of Life	Major Influence	My Experience/ Thoughts/Relationship
Childhood		
Teen Years		
College Days		
Adult Life		

Session One   13

Facts About Jesus

• The birth of Jesus _____ history.

• _____-_____ of all people on earth claim to be Christians.

• The name of Jesus has become _____, even used as a _____ _____.

The perceptions we have of Jesus have been muddied by:

• _____

• _____

• _____

And yet, the question remains, "_____ _____ _____ _____?"

a charismatic, a rabbi, a peasant Jewish Cynic, a Pharisee, an anti-Pharisee, an eschatological prophet, et cetera.

❖ POOR ANALOGIES

Different individuals often draw analogies of Jesus based on their own experiences—as an athlete (pick whichever sport you favor), as a pilot, as a teacher, et cetera.

❖ And yet, the question remains, "WHO WAS THIS JESUS?"

Bible Study (5–10 minutes)

Participant's Guide page 14

As we consider all of this information, let's turn to the Bible for a frame of reference. A short Bible study is on page 14 of your Participant's Guide. Let's get into groups of four and work through these questions. We only have a short time to finish this exercise, but the time we take will help give us a clearer picture of Jesus.

Give the groups 5–10 minutes to get together and share (depending on how much time you have left in the session). Let them know when they have 1 minute remaining.

Summary (1 minute)

Participant's Guide page 15

Okay, let's summarize what we've covered in this session. Turn to page 15 in your Participant's Guide.

Today we've taken a look at the various ways Jesus has been perceived and some of the influences on those perceptions. We've also been introduced to Philip Yancey and the film approach we'll be using throughout this course. The bottom line is for each one of us to answer the question, "Who is this man, Jesus?"

As you can see, in addition to the session summary, there is also a suggested reading passage for you if you would like to explore this topic in greater depth.

In the next session we will talk about the birth of Jesus.

Planning Notes   *Kay, Karen + Patty*

Lynne – 3 friends who are made widows... that she
          can respond to help them

Brooke – Her dad was laid off recently... can't afford
          to retire.. pray for something to open

Cammie – Scott and his deployment

Scott – My sister is pregnant w/ 2nd child.. healing
        in marriage to African American... Christine

Tom – Jaelynn *co-worker younger* – lost her sister to cancer – prayer for
      her family... Tony (Cammie) on third deployment

Susie – Bill Johnson *brain tumor* ... cancer... prayer for him

Susan – Cornerstone is closing... what will replace this?

Camille – ~~Troy~~ Troy Leander, first cousin once removed... on
          drugs all his life ... prayer for his recovery

JoAnn – Car issues

Facts About Jesus

- The birth of Jesus _____ history.

- _____-_____ of all people on earth claim to be Christians.

- The name of Jesus has become _____,
  even used as a _____ _____.

The perceptions we have of Jesus have been muddied by:

- _____

- _____

- _____

And yet, the question remains, "_____ ____ ____ ____
_____?"

Bible Study

1. Read Mark 6:1–6. What does this passage tell us about Jesus?

2. Do you think people today have any clearer picture of who Jesus is
   than did the people in his day? How do you think Jesus feels about
   the confusing portrait presented in today's church or by some individuals?

3. What impact do you think this type of study may have on your perceptions of who Jesus is? What do you hope might happen in this
   study as you take a new look at Jesus?

4. What scares you most about getting to know the real Jesus?

Summary

In this session we:

- Looked at the various ways people perceive Jesus.

- Were introduced to Philip Yancey and the film approach used
  throughout this course.

- Learned that the bottom line is for each of us to answer the question, "Who is this man, Jesus?"

Suggested Reading

For more thoughts on this session's topic, read
"The Jesus I Thought I Knew," chapter 1
of *The Jesus I Never Knew*.

Session Two:
Birth: The Visited Planet

Before You Lead

Synopsis

Sorting through a stack of Christmas cards, I notice that all kinds of symbols and sentiments have edged their way into the Christmas celebration. But when I compare today's Christmas cards to the gospel accounts of the first Christmas, I hear a very different tone. In the Gospels, I sense mainly disruption at work. Mary was a pregnant teenager and a virgin! The news an angel brought couldn't have been entirely welcome to Mary or Joseph, considering the close-knit Jewish community in which they lived. In contrast to what the cards would have us believe, Christmas did not sentimentally simplify life on planet earth.

The facts of Christmas, rhymed in carols, recited by children in church plays, illustrated on cards, have become so familiar that it is easy to miss the message behind the facts. We observe a mellow, domesticated holiday purged of any hint of scandal. Above all, we purge from it any reminder of how the story that began at Bethlehem turned out at Calvary. After reading the birth stories once more, I ask myself, *If Jesus came to reveal God to us, then what do I learn about God from that first Christmas?*

Session Outline

   I. Introduction
     Welcome
     Prayer
     Review

   II. Warm-Up
     A Christmas-Card Christmas

   III. Content
     Video Vignette
     Small Group Discussion
     Bible Study

   IV. Summary
     Dramatic Reading (Note: You need to find someone to read this for you!)
     Conclusion

Materials

Christmas cards for the warm-up: You will need a minimum of four different kinds of cards for this exercise and a maximum of ten if your class is of medium size. Dig out a few of your old cards (if you have them) or call a few people you know who might be "savers." If you cannot locate any cards, simply set up the warm-up exercise by asking people to "think about" the cards we send at Christmas.

An individual to read the dramatic reading that comprises the summary for this session: In order for this time to be effective, find someone in your class (or outside of the class if necessary) who can present the reading with a dramatic flair, someone very expressive who can make the presentation of the story interesting. Make sure you give the individual enough time to prepare!

Recommended Reading

"Birth: The Visited Planet," chapter 2 of *The Jesus I Never Knew*

Session Two:
Birth:
The Visited Planet

Introduction *(3 minutes)*

Welcome

> Call the group together.
> Welcome the participants to session 2 of *The Jesus I Never Knew* course: "Birth: The Visited Planet."

Prayer

Dear Jesus, thank you for coming to earth. As we look at the events surrounding your birth and childhood, we ask for an open mind and a teachable spirit. Guide our discussion as we seek to see you in a new way. In your name we pray. Amen.

Review

Last week we had an opportunity to think about our perceptions of Jesus. We took a look at how Jesus is described by those inside and outside the church and met Philip Yancey, the author of the book *The Jesus I Never Knew*. We also began to consider the question, "Who is this man, Jesus?"

> Participant's Guide page 17

Today we begin to take a look at this man Jesus at a very natural place—the beginning of his life. Throughout this session we will be taking a look at Jesus' birth. We'll identify those areas where our perceptions are perhaps clouded and try to see what we really can learn about God through the circumstances surrounding Jesus' birth.

Planning Notes

LAST WEEK:
EXPLORED OUR
PERCEPTIONS OF JESUS
AS WE STARTED THIS
STUDY/SMALL GROUP

THIS WEEK:
A DEEPER LOOK AT THE
BIRTH OF JESUS ... OUR
STARTING POINT IS
FITTINGLY CHRISTMAS

WELCOME
PRAYER (ME)
SCENE SETTER

"QUESTIONS TO CONSIDER"
 — DON'T ANSWER NOW
 — THIS IS WHAT WE WILL
TALK ABOUT/EXPLORE
W/ EACH OTHER TODAY

Session Two:
Birth:
The Visited Planet

Questions To Consider

- In what ways do our Christmas cards clarify or confuse our understanding of Christ's coming?

- What do the circumstances surrounding Jesus' birth teach us about God?

17

Warm-Up *(5 minutes)*

A Christmas-Card Christmas

Participant's Guide page 18

Turn to page 18 in your Participant's Guide. As we consider the first Christmas in Bethlehem, let's think about how Christmas is often portrayed in the twentieth century. One telltale conveyor of Christmas in our culture is our Christmas cards.

❖ What kinds of scenes are often presented on our Christmas cards?

> Pass your cards around and solicit responses from the group.
> Possible Answers: New England towns; cute animals—reindeer, chipmunks, raccoons, cardinals, mice; angels; Holy Family depicted in all kinds of ways—Precious Moments, children "with a glow," or members of the scene with halos

❖ What types of sentiments do our Christmas cards convey?

> Solicit responses from the group.
> Possible Answers: Scenes: Peace, joy, fun, greetings

❖ What kind of message about Jesus do these Christmas cards send to those who are not Christians?

> Solicit responses from the group.
> Possible Answers: No Christian message, happiness, "warm fuzzies," peace

In contrast to what our Christmas cards would have us believe, Christmas did not sentimentally simplify life on planet earth. The cheeriness of twentieth-century Christmas stands in contrast to the starkness of the Christmas of the Bible. Let's go to our video and see what Philip Yancey has observed and then take a look at two different films portraying the Christmas message. There is space for you to take notes on page 19 of your Participant's Guide.

Planning Notes

IMAGINE EXAMPLES OF
- PASS AROUND CARDS

THINK ABOUT THESE
- LOOK AT CARDS AS YOU
  CONSIDER THESE
  3 QUESTIONS

- ASK 2 PEOPLE TO ANSWER
  @ QUESTION

- WRAP UP:
  - SUMMARIZE INPUTS
  - READ CLOSING COMMENTS

- GO TO VIDEO
  (SEE PAGE 19 BEFORE
  SHOWING VIDEOS)
    ↳ NEXT PAGE

---

18   The Jesus I Never Knew Participant's Guide

A Christmas-Card Christmas

What kinds of scenes are often presented on our Christmas cards?

MANGER, ANGELS, SNOWY COUNTRYSIDE (STAR, SANTA)
(JOKES)
IN GENERAL: TRANQUIL, COMFORTABLE SETTINGS

What types of sentiments do our Christmas cards convey?

PEACE, HARMONY, JOY, (LOVE)

IN GENERAL: GOOD, POSITIVE SENTIMENTS

What kind of message about Jesus do these Christmas cards send to those who are not Christians? *(OR TO THOSE WHO ARE CHRISTIANS BUT LIMITED IN THEIR STUDY / KNOWLEDGE)*

(MANGER)   (SNOW SCENE)
HE'S A BABY; HE'S NOT A PART OF IT; SECONDARY TO
THE ANGELS ..

IN GENERAL: LIMITED CHRISTIAN / BIBLICAL MESSAGE

Content (30 minutes)

Video Vignette (approximately 10 minutes)

Participant's Guide page 19

View Video Vignette
Heaven—What is God like?
Philip Yancey—The unexpected choices God made at the first Christmas
Jesus of Nazareth—Joseph's doubts

Small Group Discussion (10 minutes)

Participant's Guide page 20

As we reflect on what we've just seen, let's get into smaller groups of four. Turn to page 20 in your Participant's Guide where there is a set of questions to guide your discussion.

We'll take about 10 minutes to work on this exercise.

Allow participants 10 minutes to discuss. Let them know when they have 1 minute left.

Bible Study (10 minutes)

Participant's Guide page 21

Let's stay in these small groups and go on to study what the Bible has to say about the birth of Jesus. Turn to page 21 in your Participant's Guide and take another 10 minutes to work through these questions.

Give the groups 10 minutes to share. Let them know when they have 1 minute remaining.

Once again, we have a great deal to think about as our preconceived ideas are challenged by what we've discussed in this session.

Planning Notes

- REVIEW GUIDANCE FOR VIDEOS

- WATCH VIDEOS

- SMALL GROUPS (GROUPS OF ~4) ... 4 GROUPS
  - ⌐ PAGE 20
  10 MINUTES { ⌐ 10 MINUTES TO DISCUSS
  - ⌐ @ GROUP PRESENT 1 QUESTION
    - ⌐ ASSIGN QUESTIONS TO GROUPS
    - DISCUSS -

- SMALL GROUPS (SAME AS ABOVE)
  - ⌐ PAGE 21
  10 MINUTES { ⌐ READ PASSAGES OUT LOUD
  - ⌐ DISCUSS QUESTIONS IN GROUPS
  - ⌐ @ GROUP PRESENT 1 QUESTION
    - ⌐ ASSIGN QUESTIONS (1, 3, 4, 6) TO GROUPS

Video Notes
Heaven

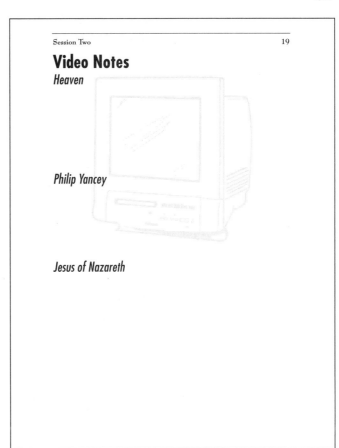

Philip Yancey

Jesus of Nazareth

Small Group Discussion

(AS PRINT)

1. What struck you as you watched the films? If Diane Keaton had asked *you,* "What is God like?" what would you have said?

  - ALL POWERFUL ... DEMANDING ... WATCHFUL ...
  BLESSING ... REWARDING/COMPASSIONATE ...
  ALL KNOWING

2. Can you see why people might have difficulty understanding how the God of the universe could come to earth as a *baby*?

  - NOT CONSISTENT WITH "GOD" VISION
  - POWERFUL vs VULNERABLE/DEPENDENT/WEAK
  - ALL KNOWING vs LEARNING THE SIMPLEST TASKS

3. Put yourself in the place of Mary or Joseph. How would you have responded to the angel's announcements?

  - HARD TO BELIEVE
  - WORRIED WHAT OTHERS WOULD THINK OF US AND OUR STORY
  - ABORTION?

4. How do you think you would have responded to Mary and Joseph's situation if you had been a member of their extended family? Critically? Skeptically? Supportively? With understanding?

  - DISBELIEF
  - SUPERFICIALLY/OBLIGATORY SUPPORTIVE

Bible Study

Read: Matthew 1:18–25 (virgin conception)
Luke 2:1–20 (shepherds)
Matthew 2:1–12 (wise men)

1. How does the biblical account compare/contrast with what we saw depicted in the films? In the Christmas cards?

- CHRISTMAS DID NOT SIMPLIFY LIFE ... IT DIVIDED THE WORLD
- IT WAS NOT A PEACEFUL TIME, BUT A TIME OF MENACE AND POVERTY (TAXES .. TERROR, HEROD) .. FEAR (PONTIUS PILATE)

2. Which aspect of the story seems most incredible to you? Why?

  - VIRGIN CONCEPTION HARD TO "BELIEVE" ESPECIALLY AS COMMON AS SIN WAS

3. What new idea have you had today concerning Jesus' birth?

- MARY WAS THE FIRST TO ACCEPT JESUS FOR WHO HE IS
- THE CONTRAST OF MY DEFINITION OF GOD/SAVIOR TO GODS
  2000S USE OF A BABY ...

4. If Jesus were born in the 1990s, what set of circumstances would parallel those of 2000 years ago?

- SIN IS ON THE RISE   - WE NEED A GUIDE TO STEER
- TERROR HAS SPAWNED FEAR   OUR CONDUCT

5. In what ways do you think Jesus was a typical child? In what ways was he different?

6. What do we learn about God from the birth of Jesus?

- WISE
- HAS FORCED US TO HAVE FAITH BY TESTING OUR OWN PRECONCEIVED NOTIONS OF WHAT A GOD/SAVIOR IS SUPPOSED TO BE
(HUMBLE, APPROACHABLE, UNDER DOG, COURAGEOUS)

Summary *(8 minutes)*

Today we've considered the birth of Christ—how God came to become one of us. As you continue to examine your own perceptions of the life of Jesus, let's conclude this session by listening to an excerpt from J. B. Phillips's book *New Testament Christianity*. This is a fantasy, but it does show us how amazing it is that God came to earth as a man.

> Dramatic Reading—See instructions in the materials list in the pre-session information. The reading is found at the end of the session material.

> Participant's Guide page 22

Why Jesus came to earth is really beyond our comprehension! In reflecting today on Jesus' birth, we've considered everything from Christmas cards to films to Scripture to an imagined conversation in heaven. Throughout this next week continue to consider what we learn about God from the circumstances surrounding the coming of Jesus to our world.

The second chapter of Philip Yancey's book, "Birth: The Visited Planet," will give you additional information and ideas as you explore this topic.

The Visited Planet

Once upon a time a very young angel was being shown round the splendour and glories of the universes by a senior and experienced angel. To tell the truth, the little angel was beginning to be tired and a little bored. He had been shown whirling galaxies and blazing suns, infinite distances in the deathly cold of interstellar space, and to his mind there seemed to be an awful lot of it all. Finally he was shown the galaxy of which our planetary system is but a small part. As the two of them drew near to the start which we call our sun and to its circling planets, the senior angel pointed to a small and rather insignificant sphere turning very slowly on its axis. It looked as dull as a filthy tennis-ball to the little angel, whose mind was filled with the size and glory of what he had seen.

"I want you to watch that one particularly," said the senior angel, pointing with his finger.

"Well, it looks very small and rather dirty to me," said the little angel. "What's special about that one?"

"That," replied his senior solemnly, "is the Visited Planet."

"Visited?" said the little one. "You don't mean visited by—?"

"Indeed I do. That ball, which I have no doubt looks to you small and insignificant and not perhaps overclean, has been visited by our young Prince of Glory." And at these words he bowed his head reverently.

Planning Notes

— SHARE THE READING --

    ↳ A "FANTASY" READING

    ↳ A WAY OF VIEWING
       OUR WORLD AND
       JESUS AND GOD IN
       A DIFFERENT CONTEXT

    ↳ GO AROUND THE ROOM
       ↳ 3 SENTENCES @

---

22   The Jesus I Never Knew Participant's Guide

Summary

In this session we:

- Explored some of the ways our Christmas cards clarify and confuse our understanding of Christ's coming.

- Identified what the circumstances surrounding Jesus' birth teach us.

Suggested Reading

For more thoughts on this session's topic, read
"Birth: The Visited Planet," chapter 2
of *The Jesus I Never Knew*.

"But how?" queried the younger one. "Do you mean that our great and glorious Prince, with all these wonders and splendours of His Creation, and millions more that I'm sure I haven't seen yet, went down in Person to this fifth-rate little ball? Why should He do a thing like that?"

"It isn't for us," said his senior a little stiffly, "to question His 'why's,' except that I must point out to you that He is not impressed by size and numbers, as you seem to be. But that He really went I know, and all of us in heaven who know anything know that. As to why He became one of them—how else do you suppose could He visit them?"

The little angel's face wrinkled in disgust.

"Do you mean to tell me," he said, "that He stooped so low as to become one of those creeping, crawling creatures of that floating ball?"

"I do, and I don't think He would like you to call them 'creeping, crawling creatures' in that tone of voice. For, strange as it may seem to us, He loves them. He went down to visit them to lift them up to become like Him."

The little angel looked blank. Such a thought was almost beyond his comprehension.

"Close your eyes for a moment," said the senior angel, "and we will go back in what they call Time."

While the little angel's eyes were closed and the two of them moved nearer to the spinning ball, it stopped its spinning, spun backwards quite fast for a while, and then slowly resumed its usual rotation.

"Now look!" And as the little angel did as he was told, there appeared here and there on the dull surface of the globe little flashes of light, some merely momentary and some persisting for quite a time.

"Well, what am I seeing now?" queried the little angel.

"You are watching this little world as it was some thousands of years ago," returned his companion. "Every flash and glow of light that you see is something of the Father's knowledge and wisdom breaking into the minds and hearts of people who live upon the earth. Not many people, you see, can hear His voice or understand what He says, even though He is speaking gently and quietly to them all the time."

"Why are they so blind and deaf and stupid?" asked the junior angel rather crossly.

"It is not for us to judge them. We who live in the Splendour have no idea what it is like to live in the dark. We hear the music and the Voice like the sound of many waters every day of our lives, but to them—well, there is much darkness and much noise and much distraction upon the earth. Only a few who are quiet and humble and wise hear His voice. But watch, for in a moment you will see something truly wonderful."

Planning Notes

Summary

In this session we:

- Explored some of the ways our Christmas cards clarify and confuse our understanding of Christ's coming.

- Identified what the circumstances surrounding Jesus' birth teach us.

Suggested Reading

For more thoughts on this session's topic, read
"Birth: The Visited Planet," chapter 2
of *The Jesus I Never Knew.*

The earth went on turning and circling round the sun, and then quite suddenly, in the upper half of the globe, there appeared a light, tiny but so bright in its intensity that both the angels hid their eyes.

"I think I can guess," said the little angel in a low voice. "That was the Visit, wasn't it?"

"Yes, that was the Visit. The Light Himself went down there and lived among them; but in a moment, and you will be able to tell that even with your eyes closed, the light will go out."

"But why? Could He not bear their darkness and stupidity? Did He have to return here?"

"No, it wasn't that," returned the senior angel. His voice was stern and sad. "They failed to recognize Him for Who He was— or at least only a handful knew Him. For the most part they preferred their darkness to His Light, and in the end they killed Him.

"The fools, the crazy fools! They don't deserve——"

"Neither you nor I, nor any other angel, knows why they were so foolish and so wicked. Nor can we say what they deserve or don't deserve. But the fact remains, they killed our Prince of Glory while He was Man amongst them."

"And that I suppose was the end? I see the whole Earth has gone black and dark. All right, I won't judge them, but surely that is all they could expect?"

"Wait, we are still far from the end of the story of the Visited Planet. Watch now, but be ready to cover your eyes again."

In utter blackness the earth turned round three times, and then there blazed with unbearable radiance a point of light.

"What now?" asked the little angel, shielding his eyes.

"They killed Him all right, but He conquered death. The thing most of them dread and fear all their lives He broke and conquered. He rose again, and a few of them saw Him and from then on became His utterly devoted slaves."

"Thank God for that," said the little angel.

"Amen. Open your eyes now, the dazzling light has gone. The Prince has returned to His Home of Light. But watch the Earth now."

As they looked, in place of the dazzling light there was a bright glow which throbbed and pulsated. And then as the Earth turned many times little points of light spread out. A few flickered and died; but for the most part the light burned steadily, and as they continued to watch, in many parts of the globe there was a glow over many areas.

"You see what is happening?" asked the senior angel. "The bright glow is the company of loyal men and women He left behind, and with His help they spread the glow and now lights begin to shine all over the Earth."

"Yes, yes," said the little angel impatiently, "but how does it end? Will the little lights join up with each other? Will it all be light, as it is in heaven?"

Planning Notes

- SOLICIT PRAYER/PRAISE
  REQUESTS

- CLOSING PRAYER (VOLUNTEER)

- COLLECT $10 TO SUSAN

Summary

In this session we:

- Explored some of the ways our Christmas cards clarify and confuse our understanding of Christ's coming.

- Identified what the circumstances surrounding Jesus' birth teach us.

Suggested Reading

For more thoughts on this session's topic, read
"Birth: The Visited Planet," chapter 2
of *The Jesus I Never Knew.*

- Candle to fuel better (30 min)
- Susan: Scott Karen arriving in Iraq/safe travel... miss him
- Lynn: Karen's best friend d-i-l struggling w/ stomach infection
- Cammie: Niece Andrea for discernment
- Dave: Son David Ryan — injury and job search... no medical or workman's comp.. his wife Renee is questioning God given the situation. Jeff and Shanna friends going back to KY looking for jobs and work in Christian life... Dave's unspoken prayer (and praise for God's response to unspoken prayer)
- Pat: Pastor George w/ his son Todd (cancer) and Pat's wife pink slip at work... unspoken prayer for Pat (job stress)
- John/Bruce: Jason Varon — chemo — scan.

His senior shook his head. "We simply do not know," he replied. "It is in the Father's hands. Sometimes it is agony to watch and sometimes it is joy unspeakable. The end is not yet. But now I am sure you can see why this little ball is so important. He has visited it; He is working out His Plan upon it."

"Yes, I see, though I don't understand. I shall never forget that this is the Visited Planet."

Planning Notes

Summary

In this session we:

- Explored some of the ways our Christmas cards clarify and confuse our understanding of Christ's coming.

- Identified what the circumstances surrounding Jesus' birth teach us.

Suggested Reading

For more thoughts on this session's topic, read "Birth: The Visited Planet," chapter 2 of *The Jesus I Never Knew*.

Session Three:
Background: Jewish Roots and Soil

Before You Lead

Synopsis

As a boy growing up in a WASP community in Atlanta, Georgia, I did not know a single Jew. Not until my early twenties did I befriend a Jewish photographer, who disabused me of many notions about his race. He described what it was like to lose twenty-seven members of his family to the Holocaust. He acquainted me with Elie Wiesel, Chaim Potok, Martin Buber, and other Jewish writers, and after these encounters I began reading the New Testament through new eyes. How could I have missed it! Jesus' true-blue Jewishness leaps out from Matthew's very first sentence, which introduces him as "the son of David, the son of Abraham."

Martin Buber said, "We Jews know [Jesus] in a way—in the impulses and emotions of his essential Jewishness—that remains inaccessible to the Gentiles subject to him." Those of us who are Gentiles face the constant danger of letting Jesus' Jewishness, and even his humanity, slip away. In historical fact, we are the ones who have co-opted *their* Jesus. I can no more understand Jesus apart from his Jewishness than I can understand Gandhi apart from his Indianness. I need to go back, way back, and picture Jesus as a first-century Jew with a phylactery on his wrist and Palestinian dust on his sandals.

I learned many things as I examined more closely the fact that Jesus was a Jew:

- For Jews who considered the name Jesus common, like "Bob" or "Joe" today, and who did not pronounce the Honorable Name of God, the idea that an ordinary person with a name like Jesus could be the Son of God seemed utterly scandalous.

- Within a generation after Jesus lived, Roman soldiers razed Jerusalem. The young Christian church accepted the destruction of the temple as a sign of the end of the covenant between God and Israel, and after the first century very few Jews converted to Christianity. Christians appropriated Jewish Scriptures, renaming them the "Old Testament," and put an end to most Jewish customs.

- Sepphoris was a gleaming city just three miles north of Nazareth. This city served as the capital of Galilee, second in importance only to Jerusalem. Not once, however, do the Gospels record that Jesus visited or even mentioned the city. He gave centers of wealth and political power a wide berth.

- At the time of Jesus' birth, Palestine was quiet under the iron thumb of Herod the Great. Years of long wars with Rome had drained both the spirit and the resources of the Jews.

- Jesus managed to confound and alienate each of the major groups in Palestine: Essenes, Zealots, the Sanhedrin, Sadducees, Pharisees. For all their differences, these groups shared one goal: to preserve what was distinctively Jewish, no matter what. To that goal, Jesus represented a threat. He held out another way, different from their choices of either separation or collaboration with Rome. His focus was on the kingdom of God.

  As a member of a minority race, how would I have responded to oppression by the mighty Roman Empire? What kind of Jew would I have made in the first century? Would Jesus have won me over?

Session Outline

  I. Introduction
     Welcome
     Prayer
     Review

  II. Warm-Up
     Jewish Culture

  III. Content
     Video Vignette
     Class Response
     Religious Leaders Within the Jewish Community
     Small Group Discussion

  IV. Summary
     Review

Materials

  No additional materials are needed for this session.

Recommended Reading

  "Background: Jewish Roots and Soil," chapter 3 of *The Jesus I Never Knew*

Session Three:
Background: Jewish Roots and Soil

Introduction *(3 minutes)*

Welcome

> Call the group together.
> Welcome the participants to session 3 of *The Jesus I Never Knew* course: "Background: Jewish Roots and Soil."

Prayer

Dear Jesus, thank you for coming into this world. As we consider your Jewish heritage, open our minds to new ideas and challenges. Help us to understand the times in which you lived on earth and to apply the lessons of yesterday to the situations of today. Thank you for this opportunity to come together and to learn more about you. For we gather in your name. Amen.

Review

For the past two weeks we've been discussing the life of Jesus and looking at that life from a new perspective. We've used films and Scripture to identify our perceptions and ideas concerning the life of Christ, and hopefully our understanding of him is being challenged and expanded. Last week we looked at the birth of Christ and how we often do not have a clear understanding of what the first Christmas involved. Today we're going to take a look at Jesus' life from another perspective—his Jewish heritage.

Warm-Up *(5–10 minutes)*

Jewish Culture

> Participant's Guide page 23

Today's session will help us identify how much—or little!—we know about Jewish culture. We'll also learn about the political and religious climate in Palestine during Jesus' lifetime and consider how we might have responded

Planning Notes

- WELCOME
  - HOW WAS THE WEEK?
  - SCOTT THIS WEEK? NEXT?
  - PRAYER REVIEW / UPDATE

- LET US OPEN WITH A PRAYER
  - ROAD (✻)

- REVIEW
  - WHEN WE STARTED, WE CONSIDERED OUR PERCEPTIONS OF JESUS... A BASELINE OF OUR OWN UNDERSTANDING

  - LAST WEEK WE TOOK A DEEPER LOOK AT THE BIRTH OF JESUS... THE CONTEXT OF HIS TIME, PLACE AND MEANING

  - THIS WEEK WE CONSIDER HIS HERITAGE... HIS CULTURAL FOUNDATION... AND HOW WELL WE MIGHT UNDERSTAND IT... AND HOW HE FIT "THE MOLD" OF BEING JEWISH IN HIS TIME

  - AS WE SHARE TIME AND THOUGHTS KEEP THESE QUESTIONS IN MIND . . . .
    - WE'LL EXPLORE MORE FULLY TODAY

Session Three:
Background: Jewish Roots and Soil

Questions To Consider

- How much do I know about Jewish culture (and therefore Jesus' Jewishness)?

- When Jesus was on earth, what was the religious/political climate in Palestine?

- How would I have responded to the religious pressure in Jesus' day?

(READ ALOUD)

↳ NEXT PAGE

23

to Jesus and his message if we had been confronted by him given the same set of circumstances.

> Participant's Guide page 24

 Turn to page 24 in your Participant's Guide. The warm-up exercise today is designed to help us identify how much we know—or think we know—about Jewish culture. Let's take a few minutes to work our way through these questions together.

> Solicit responses from the group to the following questions.

❖ Do you know someone who is Jewish? Describe that individual. What do you appreciate about his or her Jewish heritage?

❖ What are some of the stereotypes or misconceptions about Jews?

❖ If you are Jewish, what has been your experience with people who are not Jewish? Have you ever felt prejudice from non-Jewish Christians? Even if you are not Jewish, have you ever been in a position in which you have felt like a member of a minority?

❖ Share with the class your knowledge of one Jewish custom or holiday.

Content (30–35 minutes)

Video Vignette (approximately 10 minutes)

> Participant's Guide page 25

Philip Yancey has a few interesting observations about Jesus' Jewishness. Let's view today's video segment, which also contains a portrayal of Jesus' rejection by his hometown, as well as an interesting retelling of the Good Samaritan story.

> View Video Vignette
>
> *Philip Yancey*—Jesus was so very Jewish and yet he was persecuted for not measuring up to Messiah expectations.
>
> *Gospel Road*—Jesus rejected by his hometown
>
> *Cotton Patch Gospel*—The Good Samaritan story, retold. This is set in rural Georgia, not Palestine.

Class Response (5 minutes)

> Solicit responses from the group to the following questions.

Planning Notes

- TURN TO PAGE 24   (GROUP TIME #1)

  - LET'S BREAK INTO 4 GROUPS AND DISCUSS THE QUESTIONS ON THIS PAGE
  - TAKE 5-10 MINUTES (I'LL GIVE YOU A ONE MINUTE HEADS UP)
  - PURPOSE IS TO BASELINE YOUR KNOWLEDGE AND PERCEPTIONS OF THE JEWISH CULTURE
  - ⊛ — EACH GROUP WILL SHARE W/ THE REST OF US WHAT THEY FOUND MOST INSIGHTFUL OR SURPRISING FM THEIR DISCUSSION

- WATCH THE VIDEOS   (30-35 MINUTES)
  - QUICK SUMMARY ⎬
  - ⊛
  - TAKE NOTES IF DESIRED ON PG 25

Jewish Culture

Do you know someone who is Jewish? Describe that individual. What do you appreciate about his or her Jewish heritage?

- YES. SMART, INDEPENDENT, (ARROGANT), LOOKS (ISRAELI).
- CLOSE KNIT BOND IN BEING JEWISH... HAVING THAT RELIGIOUS IDENTITY

What are some of the stereotypes or misconceptions about Jews?

- PHYSICAL CHARACTERISTICS (CURLY HAIR, LG NOSE)
- CHEAP, SAVVY IN BUSINESS, CLOSED LOOP NETWORKING

N/A If you are Jewish, what has been your experience with people who are not Jewish? Have you ever felt prejudice from non-Jewish Christians? N/A Even if you are not Jewish, have you ever been in a position in which you have felt like a member of a minority?

- YES... IN SOUTH TEXAS, HISPANICS WERE THE MAJORITY @ SCHOOL, IN TOWN AND AMONG LOCAL HIRES... MADE ME FEEL LIKE AN OUTSIDER ... NOT INCLUDED

Share with the class your knowledge of one Jewish custom or holiday.

I DON'T REALLY KNOW ANY... PASSOVER?

Video Notes
Philip Yancey

Gospel Road

Cotton Patch Gospel

1. Did Philip Yancey present any ideas that were new to you? Explain.

2. How did the scene from *The Gospel Road* make you feel? How would you have responded if you had been living in that community?

3. Do you think the parallel made in *Cotton Patch Gospel*—between Jewish racism and racism against African-Americans—is a fair one?

Religious Leaders Within the Jewish Community (10 minutes)

Participant's Guide page 26

Turn to page 26 in your Participant's Guide. The political and religious climate in Jesus' day was very much a part of Jewish culture.

◆ Eight million Jews lived in the Roman empire in Jesus' day, just over a quarter of them in Palestine itself. In many ways, the plight of the Jewish leaders resembled that of the Russian churches under Stalin. They could cooperate, which meant submitting to government interference, or they could go their own way, which meant harsh persecution. In response, Jews splintered into parties that followed different paths of collaboration or separatism.

The five major groups are listed below. I'm going to give you some information about each group and then we'll read together a passage from Matthew where Jesus specifically addresses their behavior. Take whatever notes you need to enable you to participate in the small group discussion we'll have following this information.

The first group was the ESSENES.

 The Essenes were pacifistic and withdrew into monkish communities in the desert. They were committed to purity through rules on cleanliness, diet, simplicity, and communal living.

Let's read together Matthew 6:1–4.

Have someone from the class read the Scripture passage.

How would you have responded if you were an Essene and heard Jesus speak these words?

Solicit responses from the group.

Planning Notes

- DISCUSS THE VIDEOS   Ⓐ
    - USE QUESTIONS ON PREVIOUS PAGE (46)
      AS THOUGHT STARTERS

- FULL GROUP DISCUSSION ⌐ (ALL 5 TYPES)

    - JEWS IN ROMAN TIMES = RUSSIAN CHURCHES UNDER STALIN
      ① COOPERATE ⇒ GOV'T INTERFERENCE / COMPROMISE IDEALS
      ② RESIST / PRINCIPLED ⇒ HARSH PERSECUTION

    - 5 GROUPS CAME ABOUT IN JESUS' TIMES THAT
      CAN BE DEFINED ON A LINEAR SCALE WITH
      COLLABORATION AT ONE END AND PRINCIPLED
      OPPOSITION AT THE OTHER END

    - WE'LL DISCUSS EACH WITH A SCRIPTURE
      READING TO FRAME OUR DISCUSSION

                                    (VOLUNTEER
                                     TO READ?)
                                        ↓
- ESSENES (ES'EN...) MATTHEW 6:1-4
    - ASCETIC LIFE
    - EACH COLONY HAD ITS OWN SYNAGOGUE
    - COMMON HALL FOR MEALS
    - DAILY BATHING
    - NEW MEMBERS GAVE UP ALL POSSESSIONS TO THE SECT
    - READ THE LAW OF MOSES @ MORNING AND EVENING
    - DID NOT DENY FITNESS OF MARRIAGE; BUT THEY
      ABSTAINED FM WEDLOCK, EXCEPT ONE
      PARTY AMONG THEM

    - DISCUSS: HOW WOULD YOU HAVE RESPONDED
      TO HEARING JESUS SPEAK IF YOU WERE
      AN ESSENE?
                    ↳ SEE NEXT PAGE

Video Notes
Philip Yancey

What was disturbing was that Jesus
advocating treatment (fair) applied for all
people — not just the Jews...

Gospel Road

Cotton Patch Gospel

Religious Leaders Within the Jewish Community

Eight million Jews lived in the Roman empire in Jesus' day, just over a quarter of them in Palestine itself. In many ways, the plight of the Jewish leaders resembled that of the Russian churches under Stalin. They could cooperate, which meant submitting to government interference, or they could go their own way, which meant harsh persecution. In response, Jews splintered into five parties that followed different paths of collaboration or separatism.

1. E_____ (Matthew 6:1–4)
   - GIVE TO SECT VS. TO NEEDY
   - VERY PUBLIC COMMITMENT TO ESSENE LIFE

2. Z_____ (Matthew 5:43–48)

3. S_____ (Matthew 7:1–6)

4. S_____ (Matthew 5:17–20)

5. P_____ (Matthew 5:21–26)

The next group was the ZEALOTS.

The Zealots advocated armed revolt to throw out impure foreigners; some were political terrorists, some were "morals police."

Let's read together Matthew 5:43–48.

> Have someone from the class read the Scripture passage.

How do you think the Zealots responded when they heard these words?

> Solicit responses from the group.

Next we have the SANHEDRIN.

Members of this group were collaborationists who tried to work within the system. They cooperated with Romans in scouting out any sign of insurrection. Caiaphas was the high priest of the Sanhedrin.

Jesus' words addressed to this group of leaders are found in Matthew 7:1–6.

> Have someone from the class read the Scripture passage.

If you had heard these words from Jesus, how would you have felt? What would you have done?

> Solicit responses from the group.

The fourth group was the SADDUCEES.

The Sadducees were the most blatant collaborationists. Humanistic in theology, they did not believe in an afterlife or divine intervention on this earth. They enjoyed life with many material possessions.

Let's read together Matthew 5:17–20.

> Have someone from the class read the Scripture passage.

What kind of impact do think Jesus' words had on these religious leaders?

> Solicit responses from the group.

And finally we have the PHARISEES.

The Pharisees were the popular party of the middle class. Often on the fence, they vacillated between separatism and collaboration. They held to high standards of purity and treated Jews with lower standards "as Gentiles." The Pharisees suffered their share of persecution, believed passionately in the Messiah, hesitated to follow too quickly after any impostor or miracle worker who might bring disaster on the nation, and picked their battles carefully.

Planning Notes   (VOLUNTEER)

• ZEALOTS   MATTHEW 5: 43-48
   – PARTY ORGANIZED BY JUDAS
      OF GAMALA IN OPPOSITION
      TO THE CENSUS UNDER
      QUIRINIUS (6 AD)
   – INTENSELY NATIONALISTIC
   – ARDENT, FERVENT BELIEVERS
   ⌐→ QUESTION
   ———

• SANHEDRIN (SAN' HĬ DRĬN)
   MATTHEW 7: 1-6 ← (VOLUNTEER)
   – A COUNCIL OF 70-72 MEMBERS
   – COULD CONDEMN TO DEATH BUT
      NOT EXECUTE (ONLY THE ROMANS)
   – A COUNCIL
   – JESUS, PETER, JOHN, STEPHEN
      AND PAUL WERE ALL TRIED BY IT
   – COLLABORATORS AS PART OF
      ROMAN SYSTEM
   ———

• SADDUCEES (SĂĬ ŎŎ - SĒ)
   MATTHEW 5: 17-20 ← (VOLUNTEER)
   – SOCIAL ELITE
   – DENIED DOCTRINE OF RESURRECTION,
      EXISTENCE OF ANGELS, LIFE AFTER DEATH
   – REBUKED BY JOHN THE BAPTIST
   – PERSECUTED THE APOSTLES
   – FAVORED ROME
   – RULED PRIESTHOOD FOR 200 YRS (UNTIL 70 AD)
   ———

(VOLUNTEER)

• PHARISEES (MATTHEW 5: 21-26)
   – FOLLOWED TRADITIONS OF ELDERS
   – "MOST STRAIGHTEST SECT OF OUR
      RELIGION" (PAUL)
   – NATIONAL INDEPENDENCE

Religious Leaders Within the Jewish Community

Eight million Jews lived in the Roman empire in Jesus' day, just over a quarter of them in Palestine itself. In many ways, the plight of the Jewish leaders resembled that of the Russian churches under Stalin. They could cooperate, which meant submitting to government interference, or they could go their own way, which meant harsh persecution. In response, Jews splintered into five parties that followed different paths of collaboration or separatism.

1. ESSENE _____ (Matthew 6:1–4)
   – GIVING TO SECT ALL POSSESSIONS VS. TO NEEDY ?
   – PUBLIC (VS QUIET) DEDICATION TO GOD'S LAWS ?

2. ZEALOT _____ (Matthew 5:43–48)
   – "LOVING THY ENEMY" RUNS COUNTER TO ZEALOTS NATIONALISTIC FERVOR ...
      FORCES THEM TO ACCEPT FOREIGNERS AND THOSE WHO BELIEVE DIFFERENTLY
      THAN THEY DO

3. SANHEDRIN _____ (Matthew 7:1–6) – I WOULD HAVE JUDGED JESUS
   – JUDGEMENT (FOR THE SAKE OF TEARING OTHERS DOWN AND BUILD
      UP ONESELF) WAS DECRIED BY JESUS, BUT IT WAS THE PURPOSE
      FOR BEING FOR THE SANHEDRIN (COUNCIL)

4. SADDUCEE _____ (Matthew 5:17–20) – NO IMPACT ... WOULD HAVE
                                                        BEEN DISMISSED
   – BELIEF IN HEAVEN OPPOSES VIEW THAT LIFE AFTER DEATH
      IS NOT A POSSIBILITY ... LAW OF PROPHETS ≠ LAW OF ROMANS

5. PHARISEE _____ (Matthew 5:21–26)
   – VIEW HIM AS NON TRADITIONAL JEW

(VOLUNTEER)   – NOT FANATICAL LIKE ZEALOTS, OR CONCILIATORY LIKE SADDUCEES
   – GOAL: PRESERVE TRADITIONAL JUDAISM
   – BELIEVED IN SPIRITS, ANGELS AND RESURRECTION
   – JOHN THE BAPTIST: "GENERATION OF VIPERS"
   – JESUS: "HYPOCRITES"

SEE NEXT PG →

Jesus' words to the Pharisees can be found in Matthew 5:21–26.

> Have someone from the class read the Scripture passage.

How would you have responded if you were a Pharisee and heard Jesus speak these words?

> Solicit responses from the group.

Small Group Discussion (10–15 minutes)

> Participant's Guide page 27

Turn to page 27 in your Participant's Guide. Let's try to apply the information about these different religious groups to our own lives. Break into groups of four and take approximately 10 minutes (or as much time as you have left in the session) to go through the questions.

> Allow participants 10–15 minutes to share. Let them know when they have 1 minute left.

Our time is up. It's easy to be critical of the positions the religious leaders took, but it's more difficult to ascertain how each one of us would have responded to that particular set of circumstances.

Summary (1 minute)

> Participant's Guide page 28

That concludes the session on Jesus' background. In this session we tried to clarify our views and perceptions of Jewish culture. We also identified the religious and political climate in Palestine during Jesus' life and reflected on our own response to the religious pressures in Jesus' day and in our own lives.

In the next session we will discuss the temptation of Christ before he began his public ministry.

Planning Notes

GO TO PG 27...

~5 3 GROUPS
- GROUPS OF LIFE (# GROUPS)
   - EACH GROUP WILL TALK TO 1, 2 OR 3 BUT
     REVIEW/DISCUSS ALL

- SOLICIT PRAYER/PRAISE REQUEST

- CLOSING PRAYER (VOLUNTEER)

+ 3/10 chaplains believe/accept Jesus and
   walking the walk ... for the unsaved

Dave: Couple of cpts this week to go with
   this week -- ToArmi's father and
   for ToArmi   (Joe)

Pat = Pastor George + his wife ... for job
   and safe storm (Todd)

Cauralee

Narator: Todd (her 1st cousin) for help to achieve
   freedom from drugs ... Praise for cancer
   Mary from St. Louis, IL

Susan: Brodie bystedt ... looking for a
   place for to live

Pat: Ex-husband -- scholarships - plans
   to receive treatment
                4/27 - 5/4
Susan: Matt: going to MS for work
   on Katrina victim -- Scott Kane
   and safe travels and joining us

John: Jason Varon -- scan this week

Session Three 27

Small Group Discussion

1. As Christians today respond to an increasingly secular society, do they adopt approaches similar to those of these groups? Can you think of leaders or groups today who resemble these groups of Jesus' day?

- YES, TO A DEGREE ... WE TEND TO JUDGE OTHERS, QUESTION OTHERS FOR NOT BELIEVING -- WISHING THEY WOULD
- ZEALOTS => CULTS; RADICAL ISLAM => ZEALOTS;

2. Which group do you think you would have associated yourself with during Jesus' lifetime? Which of the five groups do you have a tendency to resemble within the context of our culture? Would Jesus have won you over?

- ESSENE OR PHARISEE ... DOUBTFUL
   · COMMUNAL   · MODERATE
   · BELONGING   · NATIONALISTS
   · GOODNESS   · STRAIGHT

3. Why is it so difficult to align ourselves with Jesus' message and ministry?

- AGE OF SCIENCE AND QUICK RETURN WORKS
   AT ODDS WITH FAITH AND PATIENCE ... THERE
   ARE FEW ANSWERS THAT ARE OBVIOUS

---

28 The Jesus I Never Knew Participant's Guide

Summary

In this session we:

- Clarified our views and perceptions of Jewish culture.
- Identified the religious/political climate in Palestine during Jesus' life and learned about the five different groups of religious leaders at that time.
- Reflected upon our own response to the religious pressures in Jesus' day and in our own lives.

Suggested Reading

For more thoughts on this session's topic, read "Background: Jewish Roots and Soil," chapter 3 of *The Jesus I Never Knew*.

Matt: Ken and Stephanie's new child
(Emma) ---

Session Four:
Temptation: Showdown in the Desert

Before You Lead

Synopsis

Do we humans enjoy too much freedom? We have the freedom to harm and kill each other, to fight global wars, to despoil our planet. We are even free to defy God. Couldn't Jesus have devised some irrefutable proof to silence all skeptics, tilting the odds decisively in God's favor? As it is, God seems easy to ignore or deny.

Jesus' first "official" act as an adult, when he went into the wilderness to meet the accuser face-to-face, gave him the occasion to address these problems. Satan himself tempted the Son of God to change the rules and achieve his goals by a dazzling shortcut method. But more than Jesus' character was a stake on the sandy plains of Palestine; human history hung in the balance.

Satan tempted Jesus toward the good parts of being human without the bad: to savor the taste of bread without being subject to the fixed rules of hunger and of agriculture, to confront risk with no real danger, to enjoy fame and power without the prospect of painful rejection—in short, to wear a crown but not a cross.

Did Jesus not realize that people want more than anything else to worship what is established beyond dispute? As Fyodor Dostoevsky's Grand Inquisitor says in *The Brothers Karamazov*, "instead of taking possession of men's freedom, you increased it, and burdened the spiritual kingdom of mankind with its sufferings forever. You desired man's free love, that he should follow you freely, enticed and taken captive by you." By resisting Satan's temptations to override human freedom, the Inquisitor maintains, Jesus made himself far too easy to reject. He surrendered his greatest advantage: the power to compel belief. Fortunately, continues that sly Inquisitor, the church recognized the error and corrected it, and has been relying on miracle, mystery, and authority ever since.

If I read history correctly, many others have yielded to the very temptation he resisted; the Spanish Inquisition and the Protestant version in Geneva, Adolph Hitler, Jim Jones, David Koresh, and even today's manipulation enacted in churches by those with skills learned from politicians, salespeople, and advertising copywriters.

I am quick to diagnose these flaws, yet when I examine myself, I find that I too am vulnerable to the temptation. Sometimes I wish God used a heavier touch.

My faith suffers from too much freedom, too many temptations to disbelieve. At times I want God to overcome my doubts with certainty, to give final proofs of his existence and his concern. I also lack the willpower to resist shortcut solutions to human needs. I lack the patience to allow God to work in a slow, "gentlemanly" way. I want to compel others to help accomplish the causes I believe in. I am willing to trade away certain freedoms for the guarantee of safety and protection. I am willing to trade away even more for the chance to realize my ambitions.

When I feel these temptations rising within me, I return to the story of Jesus and Satan in the desert. Jesus' resistance against Satan's temptations preserved for me the very freedom I exercise when I face my own temptations. I pray for the same trust and patience that Jesus showed.

Outline

I. Introduction
   Welcome
   Prayer
   Review

II. Warm-Up
   What *Is* Temptation?

III. Content
   Video Vignette
   Class Response
   Bible Study
   Small Group Discussion

IV. Summary
   Review

Materials

No additional materials are needed for this session.

Recommended Reading

"Temptation: Showdown in the Desert," chapter 4 of *The Jesus I Never Knew*

Session Four:
Temptation: Showdown in the Desert

Introduction *(2 minutes)*

Welcome

> Call the group together.
> Welcome the participants to session 4 of *The Jesus I Never Knew* course: "Temptation: Showdown in the Desert."

Prayer

Heavenly Father, thank you for once again giving us the opportunity to come together and study the life of Jesus. As we look closely at the temptation he experienced in the desert, may you give us insight into the real truths of this encounter and how we may deal with the temptations we encounter daily. Give us the same patience and trust in you and your ultimate plan that Christ so powerfully demonstrated for us. Amen.

Review

In the first three sessions of this course we identified our existing ideas of who Jesus was, explored his coming into our world, and tried to discover more about his Jewish heritage. Today we're going to take a look at his life just prior to the beginning of his public ministry.

Warm-Up *(5–8 minutes)*

What Is Temptation?

> Participant's Guide page 29

This session will focus on the temptation of Jesus by Satan in the desert. As we study this particular event in Christ's life we're going to try to define temptation as we know it today, explore the true nature of Jesus' temptation

Planning Notes

Session Four:

Temptation: Showdown in the Desert

Questions To Consider

- How do we experience temptation in our world?

- What was the true nature of Jesus' temptation in the desert?

- In what ways do we face the same temptations Jesus did?

29

in the desert and study the Scriptures as we identify how we also face the same types of temptations Jesus faced.

| Participant's Guide page 30 |

Turn to page 30 in your Participant's Guide.

This first exercise is designed to help us think about temptation as we experience it on a daily basis.

❖ How would you define "temptation?"

> Solicit responses from the group.
> Possible Answers: A desire, something that tries to keep me from doing what God wants me to do, something that is morally wrong

❖ What are some of the temptations you face on a daily basis?
❖ At your job
❖ With the media—TV, movies, music, the Internet
❖ With your family
❖ In your leisure time

> Solicit responses from the group.

❖ How does our society view temptation?

> Solicit responses from the group.
> Possible Answers: Most people don't even consider it; as something trivial (like "I was tempted to have one more piece of dessert!"); as something we recognize overtly—not the subtle things that Satan often uses

As we continue to think about this topic, let's turn to page 31 in the Participant's Guide as we consider two films clips and Philip Yancey's teaching.

Content (35 minutes)

Video Vignette (approximately 10 minutes)

| Participant's Guide page 31 |

Today's video segment begins with a debate between a preacher and an agnostic and then turns to Yancey's teaching. The segment closes with another clip from *Cotton Patch Gospel*.

Planning Notes

_____

_____

_____

_____

_____

_____

_____

_____

_____

_____

_____

_____

_____

_____

_____

_____

_____

_____

_____

_____

_____

_____

_____

_____

_____

_____

_____

_____

_____

_____

_____

_____

_____

_____

---

30   The Jesus I Never Knew Participant's Guide

What *Is* Temptation?

How would you define "temptation"?

What are some of the temptations you face on a daily basis?

   At your job

   With the media—TV, movies, music, the Internet

   With your family

   In your leisure time

How does our society view temptation?

Session Four   31

Video Notes
Heaven

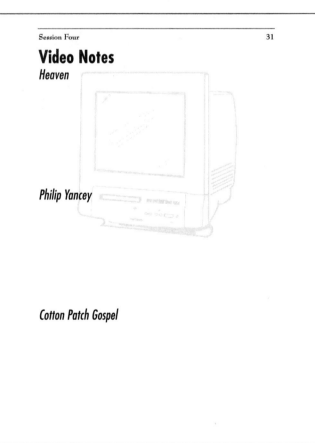

Philip Yancey

Cotton Patch Gospel

View Video Vignette
Heaven—Debate between preacher and agnostic
Philip Yancey—Nature of temptation: forcing self on others. Lessons for the church.
Cotton Patch Gospel—Temptation scene

Quite a lot of material to consider and reflect upon!

Class Response *(approximately 5 minutes)*

Solicit responses from the group to the following questions.

1. How did you feel as you watched the debate in the first film clip? What did you want the preacher to say? Have you ever felt yourself drawn into an argument about your faith?

2. Did Philip Yancey present any ideas that were new to you? Have you ever considered the "shortcut" concept he talked about?

3. In the *Cotton Patch Gospel* clip, what challenged or inspired you as you watched this unusual rendition of the temptation scene? Did anything disturb you?

Bible Study *(approximately 10 minutes)*

Participant's Guide page 32

Philip Yancey's model always calls for us to explore these topics in the light of Scripture. One of the places where we read about the Temptation in the desert is in the book of Matthew. The specific passage and a set of questions are found on page 32 of your Participant's Guide. Let's get into groups of four and work through these questions. Take 10 minutes to complete as much of this page as you can. Stay in your small groups, though, because the next exercise will also be done in these same groups.

Give the groups 10 minutes to get together and discuss. Let them know when they have 1 minute remaining.

Planning Notes

_____

_____

_____

_____

_____

_____

_____

_____

_____

_____

_____

_____

_____

_____

_____

_____

_____

_____

_____

_____

_____

_____

_____

_____

_____

_____

_____

_____

_____

_____

_____

_____

_____

Video Notes
Heaven

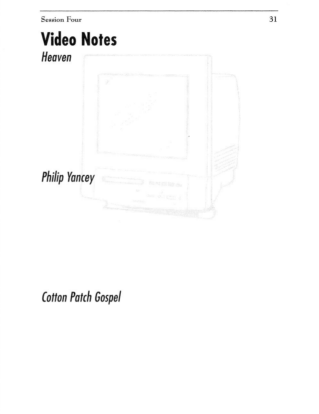

Philip Yancey

Cotton Patch Gospel

Bible Study

Read Matthew 4:1–11—"Satan Tempts Jesus in the Desert"

Satan's temptation focused on three crucial areas: (1) economics, (2) spiritual power, and (3) political power. As Malcolm Muggeridge sees it (see the exact quote in Yancey's book, pp. 72–73), the Temptation concerned the question uppermost in the minds of Jesus' countrymen: What should the Messiah look like?

A *people's* Messiah, who could turn stones into bread to feed the multitudes?

A *Torah* Messiah, standing tall at the lofty pinnacle of the temple?

A *king* Messiah, ruling over not just Israel but all the kingdoms of earth?

1. What kind of Messiah are you looking for? Do you want a God who will fix social problems and relieve the suffering in our world? Or a God who unites all the churches and clarifies the one right way? Or a God who brings worldwide peace? Or maybe you're more drawn to a God who will meet all your needs? Or a God who will guarantee your health and safety? Or a God who will cause others to respect and acclaim you? Is there anything wrong in having these hopes or expectations of God?

2. What do Jesus' responses to Satan tell us about how we are to respond to temptation?

Small Group Discussion *(approximately 10 minutes)*

Participant's Guide page 33

Let's go on to the next set of discussion questions. On page 33 we have a quote from Philip Yancey's book to give us a frame of reference for a final discussion of the temptation of Jesus.

❖ I want God to take a more active role in my personal history. I want quick and spectacular answers to my prayers, healing for my diseases, and protection and safety for my loved ones. I want a God without ambiguity, one to whom I can point for the sake of my doubting friends.

❖ When I think these thoughts, I recognize in myself a thin, hollow echo of the challenge that Satan hurled at Jesus two thousand years ago. God resists those temptations now as Jesus resisted them on earth, settling instead for a slower, gentler way.

In your same groups, take approximately 10 minutes to answer the following questions on this page.

Give the groups 10 minutes to get together and discuss. Let them know when they have 1 minute remaining.

Summary *(1 minute)*

Participant's Guide page 34

This session was packed with a great deal of information and thought-provoking discussion. We began by identifying some of the day-to-day things that tempt us; we discovered that the true nature of Jesus' temptation in the desert was the possibility of taking a "shortcut" to what was rightfully his; and we evaluated our lives in light of what tempted Jesus—specifically, a desire to meet our physical needs and desires, obtain possessions and power, and feed our pride.

The suggested reading is chapter 4 of Yancey's book. This chapter covers in greater depth some of the topics we discussed in class today, along with additional ideas.

In the next session we'll try to imagine what it would have been like to actually see Jesus in action and try to consider what *we* might have noticed had we been there.

Planning Notes

_____

_____

_____

_____

_____

_____

_____

_____

_____

_____

_____

_____

_____

_____

_____

_____

_____

_____

_____

_____

_____

_____

_____

_____

_____

_____

_____

_____

_____

_____

_____

_____

Small Group Discussion

In his book, Philip Yancey writes:

> I want God to take a more active role in my personal history. I want quick and spectacular answers to my prayers, healing for my diseases, and protection and safety for my loved ones. I want a God without ambiguity, one to whom I can point for the sake of my doubting friends.
>
> When I think these thoughts, I recognize in myself a thin, hollow echo of the challenge that Satan hurled at Jesus two thousand years ago. God resists those temptations now as Jesus resisted them on earth, settling instead for a slower, gentler way.

Do you ever wish Jesus would "hurry up" his work in your life—for example, in your job, dating relationships, friendships, marriage, raising your children, volunteer work, success in your church? What makes you spiritually impatient? What do you do with that impatience? Are you tempted to compromise Jesus' way to achieve what you want?

Summary

In this session we:

• Identified some of the day-to-day things that tempt us.

• Discovered the true nature of Jesus' temptation in the desert: taking a "shortcut" to what was rightfully his.

• Evaluated our lives in light of what tempted Jesus: (1) physical needs and desires, (2) possessions and power, and (3) pride.

> ### Suggested Reading
> For more thoughts on this session's topic, read
> "Temptation: Showdown in the Desert,"
> chapter 4 of *The Jesus I Never Knew.*

Session Five:
Profile: What Would I Have Noticed?

Before You Lead

Synopsis

Movies about Jesus help bring him to life for me. As I watch these movies, and then return to the Gospels, I try to place myself in my familiar role as a journalist. What do I see? What impresses me? Disturbs me? How can I convey him to my readers?

I cannot begin where I normally begin in reporting a person, by describing what my subject looked like. No one knows. The key lies elsewhere. I move beyond physical appearance to consider what Jesus was like as a person. How would he have scored on a personality profile? Unlike many of the films about him, the Gospels present a man with charisma. He held the attention of crowds for hours and days at a time. He lived out an ideal for masculine fulfillment that nineteen centuries later still eludes many men. He cried in front of his disciples. He did not hide his fears or hesitate to ask for help. He loved to praise other people. He quickly established intimacy with the people he met. I doubt Jesus would have followed a "to do" list or appreciated our modern emphasis on punctuality or scheduling. He let himself get distracted by any "nobody" he came across. Jesus would accept almost anybody's invitation for dinner.

Jesus came to earth "full of grace and truth" (John 1:14). He spoke of God, who lavishes his grace on veterans and newcomers alike. Despite Jesus' emphasis on grace, no one could accuse him of watering down the holiness of God. Followers were drawn by the magnetic power of his words, which, in John Berryman's description, were "short, precise, terrible and full of refreshment." Jesus' statements about himself were unprecedented and got him into constant trouble.

Oddly, when I look back on Jesus' time from the present perspective, it is the very ordinariness of his disciples that gives me hope. Jesus does not seem to choose his disciples on the basis of native talent or perfectibility or potential for greatness. I cannot avoid the impression that Jesus prefers working with unpromising recruits. From such a ragtag band, Jesus founded a church that has not stopped growing in nineteen centuries.

Session Outline

   I. Introduction
      Welcome
      Prayer
      Review

  II. Warm-Up
      Characteristics of Jesus

 III. Content
      Video Vignette
      Class Response
      Bible Study

 IV. Summary
      Review

Materials

No additional materials are needed for this session.

Recommended Reading

"Profile: What Would I Have Noticed?", chapter 5 of *The Jesus I Never Knew*

Session Five:
Profile: What Would I Have Noticed?

Introduction *(3 minutes)*

Welcome

> Call the group together.
> Welcome the participants to session 5 of *The Jesus I Never Knew* course: "Profile: What Would I Have Noticed?"

Prayer

Dear Jesus, thank you for bringing us together once again to study your life in order to know you better. As we look at your life and ministry, teach us to apply the truths of your message to our own lives. Help us to be honest with ourselves and with one another as we search for an understanding of you that truly makes a difference. In your name we pray. Amen.

Review

In our last session we studied the temptation of Jesus in the desert just prior to his beginning his public ministry. We discussed temptation in the context of how we experience it today and how Jesus dealt with his confrontation with Satan. Today we're going to begin to take a look at Jesus' ministry—how it affected people when he was here on earth and how his message is interpreted and experienced today.

Warm-Up *(5–10 minutes)*

Characteristics of Jesus

> Participant's Guide page 35

In this session we're going to discuss the life of Jesus and his message. What impression do you have of who he was when he was out interacting with

Planning Notes

(2 MIN)
- WELCOME
  - HOW WAS YOUR WEEK?
  - IS SCOTT W/ US THIS WEEK?
    - PRAY FOR YOUR SAFETY
  - ANY PRAYER / PRAISE ANSWERS?
  - GOOD TO BE BACK!

(1 MIN)
- LET US OPEN WITH A PRAYER
  - READ (*)

(2 MIN)
- REVIEW
  - WE HAVE LOOKED AT OUR PERCEPTIONS AS A BASELINE FOR GETTING TO KNOW JESUS BETTER → TALKED ABOUT HIS BIRTH → THEN HIS CULTURAL "FIT" AS A JEW IN HIS TIMES. LAST WEEK WE TALKED OF TEMPTATION FOR JESUS, FOR US AND SOCIETY. (I'M SORRY I MISSED THIS AS I BELIEVE THERE IS MUCH TO BE SAID AND LEARNED ABOUT THIS)

THIS WEEK WE WILL TAKE A CLOSER LOOK AT JESUS' MINISTRY, HIS MESSAGE AND HIS LIFE.

THOUGHT STANDOUT

Session Five:
Profile: What Would I Have Noticed?

Questions To Consider

- What impressions do you have of Jesus' physical attributes, personality, and ministry?

- What characteristics of Jesus stand out?

- What does the Bible tell us about Jesus' message and ministry?

35

people? What stands out to you? What does the Bible have to teach us about his message and his ministry?

Participant's Guide page 36

Turn to page 36 in your Participant's Guide. The questions in this session will help us begin to think about what kind of picture we have of him in our mind's eye.

Solicit responses from the group to the following questions.

❖ What words would you use to characterize Jesus as you already know him?
❖ His physical attributes

Possible Answers: Strong, handsome, tall, long-hair, beard

❖ His personality

Possible Answers: Mild-mannered, pacifistic, fun-loving, outgoing, quiet, introverted/extroverted, serious, "the life of the party"

❖ His ministry

Possible Answers: Powerful, exciting, mysterious, unpredictable

❖ When in your life did you form these impressions? What/who influenced you?

Content (30–35 Minutes)

Video Vignette (approximately 10 minutes)

Participant's Guide page 37

In today's video vignette Philip explains how he has tried to put himself in the crowd of Jesus' listeners.

View Video Vignette
Philip Yancey—Putting myself in his crowd of listeners
Witnesses—"Used-to-be's" that Jesus touched

Planning Notes

(10 MIN) TURN TO PAGE 36

— PLS TAKE 5 MINUTES TO JOT DOWN
ANSWERS (SHORT) TO @ QUESTION

— ASK FOR VOLUNTEERS TO RESPOND TO
@ QUESTION ONE AT A TIME ... ASK
FOR ANY OTHER/DIFFERENT OBSERVATIONS
OR COMMENTS ~ X 4

(10 MIN) WATCH THE VIDEOS

— 1ST ONE: PHILIP YANCEY TRIES TO
PUT HIMSELF IN THE CROWD
AS A LISTENER

— 2ND ONE: TALKS TO "USED-TO-BE'S" (IN
YANCEY'S WORDS) THAT JESUS TOUCHED

— TAKE NOTES ON PG 37 IF YOU'D LIKE

— PROVIDE QUESTIONS AS PREAMBLE

TURN PG BEFORE
STARTING MOVIE

Characteristics of Jesus

What words would you use to characterize Jesus as you already know him?

His physical attributes

BROWN HAIR AND BEARD; AVERAGE TO LEAN BUILD,
HANDSOME

His personality

SERENE (90%) AND CONDEMNING (10%)...
LARGELY NON-CONFRONTATIONAL (HE ACCEPTED
THE DECISIONS OF OTHERS RE FAITH AND
ACTIONS IMPOSED W/OUT "A FIGHT")

His ministry

GOODNESS... CARE FOR OTHERS (BEFORE SELF)...
SPORADIC (W/OUT METHOD) MIRACLES

When in your life did you form these impressions? What/who influenced you?

AT A YOUNG AGE... REINFORCED WITH CHURCH
IN HS → NOW... PARENTS VALUES WERE VERY
CLOSE TO THESE SO THEY WERE A VERY
SIGNIFICANT INFLUENCE.

Video Notes

Philip Yancey

Witnesses

Class Response *(5 minutes)*

> Solicit responses from the group to the following questions.

1. <u>What impressed you most</u> about what Philip Yancey shared in this segment? <u>What did you agree with?</u> Was there <u>anything you disagreed with?</u>

2. <u>Where would you place yourself</u> in Jesus' crowd of listeners?

3. <u>How did you react to the *Witnesses* segment?</u> Did it <u>challenge, offend, encourage, surprise, inspire you?</u> <u>Did you learn anything</u> about Jesus from the skit?

Bible Study *(15–20 minutes)*

> Participant's Guide page 38

> There are eleven passages in this short study. Divide the large group into smaller groups of four to six people and have each group work on two or three of the passages (assign each group the passages you want them to do). Give the groups 5 minutes to work through the passages, and then have one person from each group share with the larger group what they have discovered.

Turn to page 38 in your Participant's Guide. We're going to take a look at what the Bible has to say about Jesus. Break into groups of four and take approximately 5 minutes to work through your passages. Choose someone in your group to share what you discover with the whole class.

> Allow participants 5 minutes to work. Let them know when they have 1 minute remaining.

> Have the groups stay together, but have one person from each group share what they have learned with the larger group.

> Participant's Guide page 39

As we can see, Jesus was a very complicated person; there were many different sides to his personality. Let's go on to page 39 in your Participant's Guide and study just one of the parables Jesus taught. Stay in your same groups and take 10 minutes to go through the questions.

Planning Notes

5 MIN - BEFORE WATCHING VIDEO, CONSIDER ✱

   — ONLY 5 MINUTES, SO ASK FOR

   ANYONE'S COMMENTS

   ① ... ANYONE HAVE A STRONG REACTION

   (AGREEING OR DISAGREEING) TO YANCEY?

   ② WHO ARE YOU IN THE CROWD?

     (ESSENE: ASCETIC LIFE / COMMUNAL / LAW OF MOSES 2 (DAILY))

     (ZEALOT: ARDENT BELIEVERS / NATIONALISTIC / "REVOLTERS")

     (SANHEDRIN: COUNCIL OF 70-72 / JUDGERS)

     (SADDUCEES: SOCIAL ELITE / DENIED ETERNAL LIFE / ANGELS)

     (PHARISEES: TRADITIONAL JUDAISM / EMPOWERED / JUDGERS)

   ③ ... ANYONE CARE TO DISCUSS THEIR REACTION?

15 MIN — 3 GROUPS ... ASSIGN READINGS ...

   — 5 MINUTES TO READ / DISCUSS

   — CHOOSE A SPOKESMAN TO SHARE WHAT YOU DISCOVER ABOUT

   WHAT THE BIBLE SAYS ABOUT JESUS

              ← 1 MINUTE WARNING   WRITE ON THE BOARD

                   1 MINUTE WARNING

15 MIN — VOLUNTEER TO READ LUKE 10:25-37 ALOUD ... → ... STAY IN GROUPS AND DISCUSS ... ASK FOR @ GROUP INPUT

Video Notes — LEVITE: DESCENDANTS OF LEVI (JACOB'S

Philip Yancey THIRD SON BY LEAH) .. ONE OF THE APOSTLES, ALSO

CALLED MATTHEW ... PRIESTS .. ONLY ONES WHO COULD

TOUCH THE ARK / THE CARE OF THE SANCTUARY

   SAMARITAN: MIXED RACE ... SOCIALLY REPUGNANT.

ACCEPTED ONLY THE BOOKS OF THE PENTATEUCH ... FROM

SAMARIA (NORTHERN ISRAEL ... CENTER OF HEROD'S SPLENDOR)

   PRIEST: A REPRESENTATIVE OF THE PEOPLE

TO GOD ... LINEAL DESCENDANT OF AARON .. IN

NEW TESTAMENT TIMES, PRIEST CAME FROM SADDUCEES.

JEWISH PRIESTHOOD ENDED IN 70 AD W/ DESTRUCTION

Witnesses

THESE WILL HELP TO FRAME

THIS DISCUSSION AND OUR

DISCUSSION ON PG 39 LATER

     OF JERUSALEM.

Bible Study

As you read the following Scripture passages, give just a word or phrase to describe the emotions or personality characteristics Jesus displays.

ANGUISHED — Matthew 27:46 → NOT QUESTIONING GOD .. FIRST LINE
  FROM PSALM 22 ... EXPRESSION OF ANGUISH
  FOR TAKING ON SINS OF THE WORLD

DEVOTED ① Mark 1:40-41
MIRACLE CURE ... LEPROSY = UNCLEAN / NOT ALLOWED TO PARTICIPATE
IN RELIGIOUS COMMUNITY ... TOUCHING A LEPER MADE YOU UNCLEAN, TOO

DEFIANT — Mark 3:1-5
IN RIGHTEOUSNESS JESUS HEALS ON THE SABBATH WHICH WAS
  FORBIDDEN ... CHALLENGED THE PHARISEES

CARING — Mark 6:30-31
DOING GOOD WORK IS NOT EASY. REST IS REQ'D ... JESUS
  GAVE THEM THIS ...

UNSELFISH — Mark 6:34
DESPITE BEING TIRED AND LOOKING FOR A SOLITARY
PLACE, JESUS TOOK TIME TO TEACH AND SHEPHERD THOSE
IN NEED / FAITH.

② Mark 14:34-36
ACCEPTING JESUS KNEW THE AGONY AHEAD OF HIM ... THE PAIN, THE ASSUMPTION
OF THE WORLD'S SIN, SEPARATION FROM GOD ... BUT ACCEPTED IT AS GOD'S WILL

GRATEFUL — Luke 10:21
PRAISE FOR JESUS THAT THE KINGDOM OF HEAVEN IS OPEN
TO ALL ... EQUAL ACCESS THROUGH "CHILDLIKE TRUST"

SADDENED — Luke 19:41-44
JESUS ENTERS JERUSALEM ... FORETELLS OF ITS DESTRUCTION
IN 70 AD ... FOR THE CROWD'S REJECTION OF JESUS

③ Luke 23:34
FORGIVING JESUS FORGIVES (ASKED GOD TO FORGIVE) US OUR SINS EVEN
  AS HE SUFFERED ...

INSPIRING — Luke 23:43
THE CRIMINAL HAD FAITH EVEN THOUGH IT LOOKED AS IF THE
KINGDOM WAS DESTROYED ... JESUS REWARDED HIM FOR HIS FAITH

Luke 23:46
JESUS DIES AND JOINS HIS FATHER. HIS FAITH IS
TRUSTING — NOT SHAKEN.

Bible Study (continued)

Read Luke 10:25-37—The Parable of The Good Samaritan. Try to imagine that you are hearing this story for the first time.

1. How would you have felt at the end of this story if you were:

The expert in the law who asked Jesus the question, "Who is my neighbor?" EMBARRASSED FOR FAILURE TO UNDERSTAND THE
LAW AND LESSON DESPITE BEING AN "EXPERT"

A priest, Levite, or a Samaritan, ASHAMED AS A PRIEST
AND LEVITE ... PROUD AND GOOD AS A SAMARITAN

One of Jesus' disciples,
PRIDE IN FOLLOWING JESUS AND HIS TEACHINGS. PROUD
TO BE FOLLOWING HIM

An onlooker in the crowd?
THAT I HAD BEEN TAUGHT A LESSON ... TOLD HOW TO PROCEED

① ② ③

2. How do you typically respond to those around you who are in need: physically, spiritually, emotionally?
①/③: ASSIST ... LEND COUNSEL ... SUPPORT
②: TOO QUIET ... "PRIVATE MATTER" ... NOT SUPPORTING

3. As our study progresses and Jesus continues to reveal himself, are you attracted to him? His personality? His message? Would you find him threatening?
YES I AM ATTRACTED BY HIM / HIS MINISTRY. I DO NOT FIND
HIM THREATENING, BUT I DO WORRY THAT HE WILL PUNISH
ME IF I DO NOT ACT AS I SHOULD ...

Allow participants 10 minutes to work. Let them know when they have 1 minute remaining.

The last question on this page really brings us back to the importance of this course. As we reflect upon Jesus' life and study the Bible carefully, we must again ask ourselves, "Who was this man, Jesus?" and more important, "What is my response to him?"

Summary (1 minute)

Participant's Guide page 40

That concludes this session. Today we reflected upon our perceptions of Jesus' physical attributes, personality, and ministry. We learned from Philip Yancey Jesus' outstanding characteristics and began to explore what the Bible has to teach us about Jesus' message and ministry.

In the next session we'll take a closer look at Jesus' message as we study the Beatitudes and their implication for our lives today.

PRAYERS/PRAISE 5/4

- DAVE CONNORY - CAR STOLEN

- PAT VAUGHN - CARMEN - BI POLAR - CO-WORKER - NEEDS TO GET MEDS RIGHT
         TRISH WILON - HER SISTER JOAN IN CAR CRASH - RECOVERY - NECK IMMOBILIZED/LIMITED

- MATT FORREST - JEREMY (SON) FOR WISDOM - FOR SCOTT'S SAFETY

- SUSAN J   - MARA HAD HER SHOTS - NO TEARS - CUT HEAD/5 STAPLES - PRAISE...

- SCOTT - THOMPSONS - PSD - COMING HOME TO FAMILY AND RECOVERY - AND FOR ~~OUR~~ THEIR FAMILIES

- PASTOR MOLLY VELTON - HUSBAND ON 3RD IRAQ DEPLOYMENT

- TRISH ABSON - MINOR

Planning Notes

- WRAP UP
  - WE'VE DISCUSSED A LOT ... HEARD DIFFERING VIEWS ... DIFFERING THOUGHTS ON WHO JESUS WAS AND HOW WE REACT TO HIM AND THOSE VIEWS

  - CONSIDER AGAIN AS WE LEAVE ~ "WHO WAS THIS MAN JESUS?" AND MORE IMPORTANTLY, "WHAT IS MY RESPONSE TO HIM?"

- SOLICIT PRAYER/PRAISE REQUESTS

- CLOSING PRAYER (VOLUNTEER)

Bible Study (continued)

Read Luke 10:25–37—The Parable of The Good Samaritan. Try to imagine that you are hearing this story for the first time.

1. How would you have felt at the end of this story if you were:

The expert in the law who asked Jesus the question, "Who is my neighbor?"

A priest, Levite, or a Samaritan,

One of Jesus' disciples,

An onlooker in the crowd?

2. How do you typically respond to those around you who are in need: physically, spiritually, emotionally?

3. As our study progresses and Jesus continues to reveal himself, are you attracted to him? His personality? His message? Would you find him threatening?

Summary

In this session we:

- Reflected upon our impressions of Jesus' physical attributes, personality, and ministry.

- Learned about Jesus' outstanding characteristics.

- Explored what the Bible has to teach us about Jesus' message and ministry.

Suggested Reading

For more thoughts on this session's topic, read:
"Profile: What Would I Have Noticed?";
chapter 5 of *The Jesus I Never Knew*.

Session Six:
Beatitudes: Lucky Are the Unlucky

Before You Lead

Synopsis

The Sermon on the Mount haunted my adolescence. I would read a book like Charles Sheldon's *In His Steps*, solemnly vow to act "as Jesus would act," and turn to Matthew 5–7 for guidance. What to make of such advice? Should I offer myself to be pummeled by the motorcycle-riding "hoods" in school? Tear out my tongue after speaking a harsh word to my brother?

Now that I am an adult, the crisis of the Sermon on the Mount still has not gone away. Though I have tried at times to dismiss it as rhetorical excess, the more I study Jesus, the more I realize that the statements contained here lie at the heart of his message. If I fail to understand his teaching, I fail to understand him.

When I covered the Beatitudes with my class at LaSalle Street Church, the Gulf War began and ended. As I prepared videotapes of Jesus delivering the Sermon on the Mount, General Norman Schwarzkopf was giving a briefing. Blessed are the strong, was the general's message. Blessed are the triumphant. Blessed are the armies wealthy enough to possess smart bombs and Patriot missiles. Blessed are the liberators, the conquering soldiers. The bizarre juxtaposition of the two speeches gave me a feeling for the shock waves the Sermon on the Mount must have caused among its original audience, Jews in first-century Palestine. "How lucky are the unlucky!" Jesus said in effect.

A few years later I attended a prayer breakfast at the White House with President Bill Clinton and eleven other evangelical Christians. We were given the opportunity to express our concerns. The question, "What would Jesus say in such a setting?" crossed my mind. Would he say, "Don't worry about the economy and jobs—the poor are the fortunate ones"? Or "Relax, sir, government oppression gives Christians an opportunity to be persecuted and therefore blessed"? I realized with a start that the only time Jesus met with powerful political leaders, his hands were tied and his back was clotted with blood. I came away from the experience puzzled afresh. What meaning can the Beatitudes have for a society that honors the self-assertive, confident, and rich?

To put the issue bluntly, are the Beatitudes true? If so, why doesn't the church encourage poverty and mourning and meekness and persecution instead of striving against them? What is the real meaning of the Beatitudes, this mysterious ethical core of Jesus' teaching?

I am not, and may never be, ready to declare, "This is what the Beatitudes mean." But gradually I have come to recognize them as important truths. To me, they apply on at least three levels.

- *Dangled promises.* The Beatitudes are not merely Jesus' nice words of consolation to the unfortunates. It is a plain fact of history that for convicts in the Soviet Gulag and slaves in America and Christians in Roman cages, awaiting their turn with the wild beast, the promise of reward was a source of hope. It keeps you alive. It allows you to believe in a just God after all.

- *The Great Reversal.* I have also come to believe that the Beatitudes describe the present as well as the future. They neatly contrast how to succeed in the kingdom of heaven with how to succeed in the kingdom of this world. The Beatitudes express quite plainly that God views the world through a different set of lenses.

- *Psychological reality.* The Beatitudes reveal that what brings us success in the kingdom of heaven also benefits us most in this life here and now. I would rather spend time among the servants of this world than among the stars. The servants clearly emerge as the favored ones, the graced ones. They possess qualities of depth and richness and even joy that I have not found elsewhere. Somehow in the process of losing their lives, they find them.

Session Outline

  I. Introduction
     Welcome
     Prayer
     Review

 II. Warm-Up
     Beati-what?

III. Content
     The Teaching of Jesus
     Scripture Reading
     Video Vignette
     Class Response
     Small Group Discussion
     Personalized Beatitudes

 IV. Summary
     Review

Materials

No additional materials are needed for this session.

Recommended Reading

"Beatitudes: Lucky Are the Unlucky," chapter five of *The Jesus I Never Knew*

Session Six:
Beatitudes:
Lucky Are the Unlucky

Introduction *(3 minutes)*

Welcome

> Call the group together.
> Welcome the participants to session 6 of *The Jesus I Never Knew* course: "Beatitudes: Lucky Are the Unlucky."

Prayer

Dear Jesus, your words challenge, confront, encourage, and comfort us. Give us wisdom today as we study the Beatitudes and help us apply them to our lives in a way we never have before. Give us courage to look deep within and to see how you would have us live. In your name we pray. Amen.

Review

In the first five sessions of the course we tried to identify who Jesus was. We not only examined our perceptions and views of him, but also looked specifically at his birth, his background, and his temptation by Satan in the desert prior to the beginning of his public ministry. Today marks the beginning of "Part Two" of this course: Why Jesus Came.

Warm-Up *(5 minutes)*

Beati-what?

> Participant's Guide page 41

In this session we're going to begin to study Jesus' message—not only to those who heard him speak while he was on earth, but also to us today. Our time today will be spent studying the Beatitudes. We'll take a look at what we've learned in the past about Jesus' teaching, discuss why the message of

Planning Notes

(5MIN) • WELCOME

— HOW WAS YOUR WEEK?

— DAVE: ANY LUCK W/ CAR?
ANY ID PROBLEMS?

— SCOTT: ADJUSTING?
SAFETY?

— MATT: HOW IS JOSEPH DOING? (SON)

— SUSAN: NO MORE STITCHES FOR MAMA?

(1MIN) • LET US OPEN WITH A PRAYER

— READ ⊛

(2MIN) • REVIEW... WE'VE LOOKED AT:

— OUR PERCEPTIONS OF JESUS

— HIS BIRTH

— HIS CULTURAL FIT AS A JEW

— HIS TEMPTATIONS

— HIS LOOKS AND HIS MESSAGE

(1MIN) • TODAY WE SPEND TIME WITH
THE BEATITUDES... OUR
DISCUSSION WILL BE SHAPED
BY THESE QUESTIONS TO
CONSIDER

• MY FIRST CHALLENGE WAS NOT
KNOWING WHAT "BEATITUDES"
MEANS... SO I LOOKED IT UP

— ANYONE WANT TO OFFER THEIR
DEFINITION/UNDERSTANDING?

Session Six:
Beatitudes: Lucky Are the Unlucky

Questions To Consider

- In the past, what has been your response to the Beatitudes?

- Why is the message of Jesus so difficult for us to grasp?

- What new insights can we gain if we look at the Beatitudes in a new way?

BEATITUDE:
BLESSEDNESS, THE NAME GIVEN TO ANY
OF THE PRONOUNCEMENTS OF BLESSINGS
GIVEN BY JESUS IN MATTHEW 5: 3-12
(THE BEGINNING OF THE SERMON ON
THE MOUNT)

Jesus is often so difficult for us to grasp, and try to gain new insights into how we can apply the Beatitudes to our lives.

Participant's Guide page 42

Turn to page 42 in your Participant's Guide. "Beati-what?" is the title for the questions found on this page. Maybe some of us have never even considered the Beatitudes and what they mean. Maybe you've read the passage in Matthew again and again but never really reflected upon how it should apply to your life today. As we turn our thoughts to the words found at the beginning of Jesus' Sermon on the Mount, let's think about these questions.

Solicit responses from the group to the following questions.

❖ What feelings/experiences have you had as you studied the Beatitudes in the past?

❖ Have you ever considered following the Beatitudes literally?

❖ Why do you think it is difficult for us to take the Beatitudes seriously? Do Christians try to follow some of the Beatitudes and let the rest go? Are these words of Jesus just nice phrases that sound good but have no practical relevance? When is the last time you seriously considered this passage of Scripture?

Content (35 minutes)

The Teaching of Jesus (3 minutes)

Participant's Guide page 43

Let's turn to page 43 in your Participant's Guide. Philip Yancey has given this topic a great deal of study and reflection. Later in this session he will amplify some of his thoughts for us on the video segment, but I would also like to highlight some of the teaching that he has included in his book.

One of his most confrontational thoughts for us is the first statement found in your Participant's Guide on page 43.

❖ Though I have tried at times to dismiss the Sermon on the Mount as RHETORICAL EXCESS, the more I study Jesus, the more I realize that the statements contained here lie at the HEART of his MESSAGE. If I fail to UNDERSTAND this teaching, I fail to understand HIM.

This is a very strong statement. What do you think would happen to our world if all Christians would respond to the Beatitudes as Yancey suggests? The heart of Jesus' message! This is a good thought for us to keep in mind throughout our study during this session.

Yancey goes on to assert:

Planning Notes

(1 MIN) • GOING A LITTLE OUT OF ORDER, LET'S
READ MATTHEW 5: 1-12 ALOUD SO WE
ALL HAVE A COMMON STARTING POINT
— ONE VERSE/PERSON GOING AROUND TABLE

(5 MIN) • ASK FOR PERSONAL THOUGHTS/COMMENTS
ON THE QUESTIONS FM PG 42
— ASK THE QUESTION/OPEN UP TO GROUP

(5 MIN) • PAGE 43 ... A BIT OF A POP QUIZ FM
THE SUMMARY OF YANCEY'S WRITING
ON THIS TOPIC

— ASK THE FILL IN THE BLANK PORTION
— THEN READ THE HIGHLIGHTED PART

RHETORICAL EXPRESSION →
HEART ... MESSAGE →

[NEXT PAGE]

Beati-what?

What feelings/experiences have you had as you studied the Beatitudes in the past?

— NEVER STUDIED BEFORE
— MIXED MESSAGE "BLESSING" "POOR IN SPIRIT" AND "MEEK" VS "RIGHTEOUSNESS" AND "MERCIFUL"
— A GUIDEBOOK FOR HOW TO ACT

Have you ever considered following the Beatitudes literally?

— NO, INSPIRATION WOULD BE A CLOSER DESCRIPTION
— NOT ALWAYS SURE HOW TO DO THIS ... HOW DO YOU BE MEEK? OR POOR IN SPIRIT?

① Why do you think it is difficult for us to take the Beatitudes seriously?
② Do Christians try to follow some of the Beatitudes and let the rest go?
③ Are these words of Jesus just nice phrases that sound good but have no practical relevance? ④ When is the last time you seriously considered this passage of Scripture?

① NOT EASILY UNDERSTOOD. CALL FOR SELFLESS ACTS. CAN APPEAR TO PLACE PERSONAL NEEDS AS SECONDARY — HARD SACRIFICES...
② ABSOLUTELY... EVERYONE DOES THIS... IMPOSSIBLE TO BE FULLY LIKE JESUS
③ THEY HAVE PRACTICAL RELEVANCE
④ TODAY, BUT RARELY EVER.

The Teaching of Jesus

Philip Yancey says: Though I have tried at times to dismiss the Sermon on the Mount as _____, the more I study Jesus, the more I realize that the statements contained here lie at the _____ of his _____. If I fail to _____ [UNDERSTAND] this teaching, I fail to understand _____ [HIM].

The Beatitudes _____ to us on at least three levels:

1. Dangled Promises—The Beatitudes give us the _____ ____ _____. They are a _____ ___ _____. They allow us to believe in a just God after all.

2. The Great Reversal—The Beatitudes describe the _____ as well as the _____. They express that God views the world through a _____ set of _____.

3. Psychological Reality—The Beatitudes reveal that what brings us success in the _____ ___ _____ also benefits us most in _____ _____.

❖ The Beatitudes APPLY to us on at least three levels.

❖ 1. Dangled Promises—The Beatitudes give us the PROMISE OF REWARD. They are a SOURCE OF HOPE. They allow us to believe in a just God after all.

The Beatitudes are not merely nice words of consolation to the unfortunate. It is a fact of history that for convicts in the Soviet Gulag and slaves in America, this type of promise could keep you alive. It gives you something to hold on to.

❖ 2. The Great Reversal—The Beatitudes describe the PRESENT as well as the FUTURE. They express that God views the world through a DIFFERENT set of LENSES.

The Beatitudes contrast how to succeed in the kingdom of heaven with how to succeed in the kingdom of this world. God's kingdom turns the tables upside down. The poor, the hungry, the mourners, and the oppressed are those who are blessed because of an innate advantage they hold over those more comfortable and self-sufficient. People who are rich, successful, and beautiful may well go through life relying on their natural gifts. People who lack such natural advantages, and hence are underqualified for success in the kingdom of this world, just might turn to God in their time of need. Human beings do not readily admit desperation. When they do, the kingdom of heaven draws near.

❖ 3. Psychological Reality—The Beatitudes reveal that what brings us success in the KINGDOM OF HEAVEN also benefits us most in THIS LIFE.

Jesus knew how life works, in the kingdom of heaven as well as in the kingdom of this world. In a life characterized by poverty, mourning, meekness, a hunger for righteousness, mercy, purity, peacemaking, and persecution, Jesus himself embodied the Beatitudes.

Scripture Reading: The Beatitudes *(2 minutes)*

With this information as a frame of reference, let's read together the Beatitudes in Matthew 5:1–12.

Read Scripture passage.

Video Vignette *(approximately 10 minutes)*

Participant's Guide page 44

In today's video segment we have a traditional portrayal of Jesus giving the Beatitudes in the film *Jesus*. Note that Jesus delivers his words while interacting with people, rather than stiffly delivering a sermon. As you listen to this actor deliver these powerful words, try to imagine how you would have felt if you had heard them for the first time directly from Jesus himself.

Planning Notes

(MIN)(CONT.)
- QUIZ (CONTINUED)

    — ASK THE FILL IN THE BLANK PART
    — THEN READ THE HIGHLIGHTED SECTIONS

    —

(10 MIN) • VIDEO
    — TRY TO IMAGINE HOW YOU WOULD
    HAVE FELT IF YOU HAD HEARD THEM
    FOR THE FIRST TIME... ESPECIALLY IN
    THE CONTEXT OF ROMAN OPPRESSION,
    EXPECTATIONS OF A MESSIAH, YOUR
    PERSONAL SUFFERING IN YOUR
    DAILY LIFE, AND WHAT YOU VALUE
    IN PERSONAL CHARACTERISTICS THAT
    DEFINE SUCCESS (E.G., STRENGTH,
    WEALTH, POWER, FREEDOMS...)

    — NOTES ON PG 44

The Teaching of Jesus EXPRESSION

Philip Yancey says: Though I have tried at times to dismiss the Sermon on the Mount as _RHETORICAL_ , the more I study Jesus, the more I realize that the statements contained here lie at the _HEART_ of his _MESSAGE_ . If I fail to _UNDERSTAND_ this teaching, I fail to understand _HIM_ .

The Beatitudes ___APPLY___ to us on at least three levels:

1. Dangled Promises—The Beatitudes give us the _PROMISE_ _OF REWARD_ . They are a _SOURCE OF HOPE_ . They allow us to believe in a just God after all.

2. The Great Reversal—The Beatitudes describe the _PRESENT_ as well as the _FUTURE_ . They express that God views the world through a _DIFFERENT_ set of _LENSES_ .

3. Psychological Reality—The Beatitudes reveal that what brings us success in the _KINGDOM OF HEAVEN_ also benefits us most in _THIS LIFE_ .

Video Notes
Jesus

Philip Yancey

View Video Vignette
Jesus—Sermon on the Mount
Philip Yancey—How do the Beatitudes make sense?

Class Response (5 minutes)

Solicit responses from the group to the following questions.

1. What were some of your thoughts as you watched the *Jesus* segment?

2. What words from Philip Yancey challenged you?

Small Group Discussion (10 minutes)

Participant's Guide page 45

Turn to page 45 in your Participant's Guide. We're going to do this exercise in small groups of four. Read the J. B. Phillips paraphrase and then discuss the questions. We'll take 10 minutes to do this exercise.

Allow participants 10 minutes to share. Let them know when they have 1 minute remaining.

It would be easy for each of us to leave the Beatitudes right here—at a more abstract place, thinking of how they can't really apply to our situations and relationships right now. However, Yancey has given us an opportunity to apply these truths personally. Let's turn to page 46 in our Participant's Guide.

Personalized Beatitudes (5 minutes)

Participant's Guide page 46

As we read through the "Personalized Beatitudes," think about how they reflect your values and behaviors. Choose one or two that you need to think about and pray about over the next week.

Read the Personalized Beatitudes aloud as a class. You may wish to have someone other than yourself read all of them, or you could have each statement read by a different person.

❖ I am blessed because in my loneliness, my fears, and my inner struggles, God has promised me a beautiful future. That promise helps me see my struggles with new eyes.

❖ I am blessed as I grieve. In the depths of my sorrow Jesus meets me and mourns with me, bringing comfort in unexpected ways.

Planning Notes

⟲ 10 MIN (CONT)
- ● VIDEO (CONT)
  - ANY THOUGHTS ON THE VIDEO?
  - HOW WOULD YOU HAVE RECEIVED THE SERMON?
  - DID YANCEY CHALLENGE YOU?

- ● SMALL GROUPS OF 3-4 PEOPLE
  - ① LOOK @ PG 45... READ AND DISCUSS IN GROUPS
    - SOLICIT COMMENTS FM @ GROUP
      FOR @ QUESTION

  - ② GO TO BOARD -- PG 116 (A "I" AND "POOR") ^HS/
    - ARE YOU MORE LIKE THIS POOR OR RICH?
    - DO YOU ACKNOWLEDGE YOUR NEEDS?
    - DO YOU DEPEND ON GOD/PEOPLE OR POSSESSIONS TO GIVE YOU SECURITY
    - BEATITUDES ⇒ GOOD NEWS OR A SCOLDING?

- ● READ ALOUD THE PERSONALIZED BEATITUDES
  - AROUND THE ROOM
  - DO THEY REFLECT YOUR VALUES/BEHAVIORS?

Video Notes
Jesus

Philip Yancey

- CHOOSE 1 OR 2 TO FOCUS ON/PRAY ABOUT THIS WEEK

Small Group Discussion

J. B. Phillips rendered this version of the Beatitudes as they apply in the kingdom of this world:

Happy are the "pushers": for they get on in the world.
Happy are the hard-boiled: for they never let life hurt them.
Happy are they who complain: for they get their own way in the end.
Happy are the blasé: for they never worry over their sins.
Happy are the slave-drivers: for they get results.
⊛ Happy are the knowledgeable men of the world: for they know their way around.
Happy are the trouble-makers: for they make people take notice of them.

1. What is your initial reaction to this paraphrase?

- ODD CHOICE OF WORDS ("PUSHERS", "HARD-BOILED")
- DO NOT AGREE WITH "CAUSE/EFFECT" (BLASÉ ≠ NEVER WORRY OVER SINS)
- NOT ALL BAD (⊛)

Ⓠ 2. These words seem to reflect the values of our culture. ② What meaning can the Beatitudes have for a society that honors the self-assertive, the confident, and the rich?

- Ⓠ I'M NOT SURE THESE REFLECT TODAY'S CULTURAL VALUES
- ② TEMPER THE ARROGANCE, SELF-SERVING TENDENCIES OF SOME... STEER US TOWARD A BETTER, MORE SELFLESS, MORAL EXISTENCE

Personalized Beatitudes

How do these statements reflect your values and behaviors? Choose one or two that you especially need to think and pray about.

- I am blessed because in my loneliness, my fears, and my inner struggles, God has promised me a beautiful future. That promise helps me see my struggles with new eyes.

- I am blessed as I grieve. In the depths of my sorrow Jesus meets me and mourns with me, bringing comfort in unexpected ways.

- I am blessed in choosing not to exalt myself. This means I get overlooked at times, but I'm living for God, not for the acclaim of men and women. Someday I'll be glad I chose the way of humility.

- I am blessed in my yearning to live as Jesus did. God is faithful to me as I ponder Jesus' righteous ways and pray for the Spirit to guide how I live and who I am.

- I am blessed because I choose to show mercy, even when others don't really deserve it. I see much in me that is undeserving, yet Jesus has been merciful again and again.

- I am blessed because I'm careful about what I do, see, read, and think about. I want to be pure because this is when I can see God most clearly. This is when I am closest to God.

- I am blessed because I long for peace among those around me. I desire to enter into the world of others to better understand and come alongside them. I'm willing to do what is uncomfortable for the sake of peace, following in the footsteps of Jesus.

- I am blessed when, because of my loyalty to Jesus, others look down on me, violate my God-given rights, lie about me with evil intent, or hurt me. This world is not my home, and persecution blesses me because it is a reminder of the kingdom of heaven that awaits me not so far away. For "no eye has seen, no ear has heard, no mind has conceived what God has prepared for those who love him" (1 Cor. 2:9).

❖ I am blessed choosing not to exalt myself. This means I get overlooked at times, but I'm living for God, not for the acclaim of men and women. Someday I'll be glad I chose the way of humility.

❖ I am blessed in my yearning to live as Jesus did. God is faithful to me as I ponder Jesus' righteous ways and pray for the Spirit to guide how I live and who I am.

❖ I am blessed because I choose to show mercy, even when others don't really deserve it. I see much in me that is undeserving, yet Jesus has been merciful again and again.

❖ I am blessed because I'm careful about what I do, see, read, and think about. I want to be pure because this is when I can see God most clearly. This is when I am closest to God.

❖ I am blessed because I long for peace among those around me. I desire to enter into the world of others to better understand and come alongside them. I'm willing to do what is uncomfortable for the sake of peace, following in the footsteps of Jesus.

❖ I am blessed when, because of my loyalty to Jesus, others look down on me, violate my God-given rights, lie about me with evil intent, or hurt me. This world is not my home, and persecution blesses me because it is a reminder of the kingdom of heaven that awaits me not so far away. For "no eye has seen, no ear has heard, no mind has conceived what God has prepared for those who love him" (1 Cor. 2:9).

Summary *(1 minute)*

Participant's Guide page 47

That concludes our session on the Beatitudes. We are now getting into the heart of why Jesus came. In this session we reflected upon our past interpretations of the Beatitudes, explored the teaching of Jesus, and discovered new insights into this very important aspect of Jesus' teaching.

In the next session we will study the remaining message of the Sermon on the Mount.

Planning Notes

- SOLICIT PRAYER/PRAISE REQUESTS

- CLOSING PRAYER/VOLUNTEER

5/11 PRAYERS:

LAURALEE: DAVE'S PERSONAL CAR SITUATION

MIKE: PRAISE FOR VOLUNTEERS

LYNN: SCOTT + IRAQ + ECONOMY + NEXT PRESIDENT

SUSAN: LESLIE ROBERTS/HOSPITAL -- CLINICAL
DEPRESSION, MIGRAINES, BLOOD CLOTS,
PNEUMONIA -- LONG TERM HEALING

PAT: · CARMEN BIPOLAR ILLNESS
PRAISE FOR TREATMENT CENTERS

MIKE: FOR JEFF -- HELP HIM/GUIDE HIM TO
BE RESPONSIBLE

Personalized Beatitudes

How do these statements reflect your values and behaviors? Choose one or two that you especially need to think and pray about.

- I am blessed because in my loneliness, my fears, and my inner struggles, God has promised me a beautiful future. That promise helps me see my struggles with new eyes.

- I am blessed as I grieve. In the depths of my sorrow Jesus meets me and mourns with me, bringing comfort in unexpected ways.

- I am blessed in choosing not to exalt myself. This means I get overlooked at times, but I'm living for God, not for the acclaim of men and women. Someday I'll be glad I chose the way of humility.

- I am blessed in my yearning to live as Jesus did. God is faithful to me as I ponder Jesus' righteous ways and pray for the Spirit to guide how I live and who I am.

- I am blessed because I choose to show mercy, even when others don't really deserve it. I see much in me that is undeserving, yet Jesus has been merciful again and again.

- I am blessed because I'm careful about what I do, see, read, and think about. I want to be pure because this is when I can see God most clearly. This is when I am closest to God.

- I am blessed because I long for peace among those around me. I desire to enter into the world of others to better understand and come alongside them. I'm willing to do what is uncomfortable for the sake of peace, following in the footsteps of Jesus.

- I am blessed when, because of my loyalty to Jesus, others look down on me, violate my God-given rights, lie about me with evil intent, or hurt me. This world is not my home, and persecution blesses me because it is a reminder of the kingdom of heaven that awaits me not so far away. For "no eye has seen, no ear has heard, no mind has conceived what God has prepared for those who love him" (1 Cor. 2:9).

Summary

In this session we:

- Reflected upon our past interpretations of the Beatitudes.

- Explored the teaching of Jesus.

- Discovered new insights into the Beatitudes.

Suggested Reading

For more thoughts on this session's topic, read
"Beatitudes: Lucky Are the Unlucky,"
chapter 6 of *The Jesus I Never Knew*.

Session Seven:
Message:
A Sermon of Offense

Before You Lead

Synopsis

The Beatitudes represent only the first step toward understanding the Sermon on the Mount. Long after I came to recognize the enduring truth of the Beatitudes, I still brooded over the uncompromising harshness of the rest of Jesus' sermon. Its absolutist quality left me gasping. "Be perfect, therefore, as your heavenly Father is perfect," Jesus said (Matt. 5:48), his statement tucked almost casually between commands to love enemies and give away money. Be perfect like God? Whatever did he mean?

I once went on a reading binge in search of the key to understanding the Sermon on the Mount, and it brought some consolation to learn I was not the first to flounder over its high ideals. Throughout history, people have found canny ways to reconcile Jesus' absolute demands with the grim reality of human delinquency.

- Thomas Aquinas divided Jesus' teaching into two levels of commitment: precepts and counsels, or requirements and suggestions.
- Martin Luther interpreted the Sermon on the Mount in light of Jesus' formula "Give to Caesar what is Caesar's, and to God what is God's" (Matt. 22:21). "Christians maintain a dual citizenship," Luther said: one in the kingdom of Christ and one in the kingdom of the world. The extremism in the Sermon on the Mount applies absolutely to Christ's kingdom but not to the world's.
- The Anabaptist movements chose a radically different approach. All such attempts to water down Jesus' straightforward commands are misguided, they said. They felt we should follow Jesus' command in the most literal way possible.
- In nineteenth-century America a theological movement called dispensationalism explained such teaching as the last vestige of the age of Law, which was soon to be displaced by the age of Grace after Jesus' death and resurrection. Hence, we need not follow its strict command.
- Albert Schweitzer, convinced the world would soon end in the apocalypse, saw the Sermon on the Mount as a set of interim demands for unusual times. Since the world did not end, we must now view those instructions differently.

Each school of thought contributed important insights, yet each also seemed to have a blind spot. Ultimately I found a key to understanding the Sermon on the Mount, not in the writings of great theologians but in a more unlikely place: the writings of two nineteenth-century Russian novelists—Tolstoy and Dostoevsky.

From Tolstoy I learned a deep respect for God's inflexible, absolute ideal. Like the Anabaptists, Tolstoy strove to follow the Sermon on the Mount literally. Sometimes he accomplished great good. His philosophy of nonviolence, lifted directly from the Sermon on the Mount, had an impact that long outlived him in ideological descendants like Gandhi and Martin Luther King Jr. Yet his intensity soon caused his family to feel like victims of his quest for holiness. His wife said, "There is so little genuine warmth about him; his kindness does not come from his heart, but merely from his principles."

Tolstoy failed to practice what he preached, and he never found peace. He found, rather, that in many ways the gospel actually adds to our burdens. Yet to his critics he replied, "If I know the way home and am walking along it drunkenly, is it any less the right way because I am staggering from side to side! If it is not the right way, then show me another way; but if I stagger and lose the way, you must help me, you must keep me on the true path, just as I am ready to support you." Despite his failures, Tolstoy's relentless pursuit of authentic faith has made an indelible impression on me. Having grown up with many whom, in my arrogance of youth, I considered frauds, Tolstoy as an author accomplished for me the most difficult of tasks: to make Good as believable and appealing as Evil.

Tolstoy could see with crystalline clarity his own inadequacy in light of God's ideal. But he could not take the further step of trusting God's grace to overcome that inadequacy. Shortly after reading Tolstoy, I discovered his countryman Fyodor Dostoevsky. He was the opposite of Tolstoy in every way, but he got one thing right: his novels communicate grace and forgiveness with a Tolstoyan force. Early in his life he was nearly executed but was spared at the last instant. He never recovered from this experience. He spent ten years in exile poring over the New Testament and emerged with unshakable Christian convictions. In prison he came to believe that only through being loved is a human being capable of love. He went on to write about grace in his novels. Alyosha, in *The Brothers Karamazov,* does not know the answer to the problem of evil, but he does know love.

These two authors helped me come to terms with a central paradox of the Christian life. From Tolstoy I learned the need to look inside, to the kingdom of God that is within me. I saw how miserably I had failed the high ideals of the gospel. But from Dostoevsky I learned the full extent of grace. Not only the kingdom of God is within me; Christ himself dwells there. There is only one way for us to resolve the tension between the high ideals of the gospel and the grim reality of ourselves: to accept that we will never measure up, but that we do not have to. We are judged by the righteousness of the Christ who lives within, not our own.

Why did Jesus give us the Sermon on the Mount? Not to burden us but to tell us what God is like. He gave us God's Ideal to teach us that we should never stop striving yet also to show us that none of us will ever reach that Ideal.

Session Outline

I. Introduction
   Welcome
   Prayer
   Review

II. Warm-Up
   Offended? Who, Me?

III. Content
   Scripture Reading: The Sermon on the Mount
   Bible Study
   Personal Application
   Video Vignette
   Class Response

IV. Summary
   Review

Materials

No additional materials are needed for this session.

Recommended Reading

"Message: A Sermon of Offense," chapter 7 of *The Jesus I Never Knew*

Session Seven:
Message:
A Sermon of Offense

Introduction (3 minutes)

Welcome

> Call the group together.
>
> Welcome the participants to session 7 of *The Jesus I Never Knew* course: "Message: A Sermon of Offense."

Prayer

Dear Jesus, once again we thank you for the opportunity to come together to study your life and your Word. As we look today at the message of the Sermon on the Mount, help us to remember that you said, "My yoke is easy and my burden is light." May we not get bogged down in the difficulty of your words but remember that you live in us, empowering us to be you in our world. Teach us what it means to be your disciples. Amen.

Review

In our last session we began to look at Jesus' message specifically as he gave it in the Sermon on the Mount. Session 6 allowed us to reflect upon the Beatitudes and what they have to say to us today. This session will give us the opportunity to look at the remainder of the Sermon on the Mount, a message we all need to consider.

Warm-Up (5 minutes)

Offended? Who, Me?

> Participant's Guide page 49

In this session we're going to take a look at what offends people today and then think about how Jesus' message was an offense to many. We're also going to read the Sermon on the Mount as a whole and then take some time

Planning Notes

_____
_____
_____
_____
_____
_____
_____
_____
_____
_____
_____
_____
_____
_____
_____
_____
_____
_____
_____
_____
_____
_____
_____
_____
_____
_____
_____
_____

Session Seven:
Message: A Sermon of Offense

Questions To Consider

- What kinds of things offend people?

- Does the Sermon on the Mount have anything to say to us today?

- How do we maintain high ideals while offering a safety net of grace?

49

to reflect on what it says to us today. Finally, we'll consider how we can maintain the high ideals that Jesus set before us while offering the safety net of grace that he so clearly advocated.

> Participant's Guide page 50

Turn to page 50 in your Participant's Guide. This session's title is *Message: A Sermon of Offense.*

◆ If you are familiar with the Sermon on the Mount, have you ever considered its message "offensive"?

> Solicit responses from the group.

◆ In our culture, what messages from the church do people often find offensive?

> Solicit responses from the group.
> Possible Answers: Anything to do with asking for money; anything that offers an absolute to a behavior, such as the Catholic church's position on abortion; any disapproval of sexual behavior; the idea of Jesus as the only way to heaven is offensive

◆ In the church, what kinds of things offend people? What kinds of things offend *you* (honestly!)?

> Solicit responses from the group.
> Possible Answers: any of the answers from the previous question(!); the music; the greeters; the ushers; the way the minister delivers his message (too upbeat, too serious, etc., etc., etc.); the church board; the youth ministry (or any other specific ministry); the extensive building and use of money

When we talk about some of these issues in light of the Sermon on the Mount, some of them seem almost ridiculous in light of the serious topics Jesus undertook to teach on. Others of these issues were "hot topics" in Jesus' day, too.

Planning Notes

Offended? Who, Me?

If you are familiar with the Sermon on the Mount, have you ever considered its message "offensive"?

In our culture, what messages from the church do people often find offensive?

In the church, what kinds of things offend people? What kinds of things offend *you* (honestly!)?

Content *(35 minutes)*

Scripture Reading *(5 minutes)*

❖ How many of you have read the Sermon on the Mount in its entirety?

> Ask for a show of hands.

In addition to the Beatitudes, Jesus addresses eighteen different topics in the Sermon on the Mount. Many of us are probably familiar with these passages, but we've never taken a look at them in the context of being part of the Sermon on the Mount. Open your Bibles to Matthew 5:13. To give us the proper framework for the remainder of this session, we're going to take the time to read the Sermon on the Mount together, reading from Matthew 5:13 through chapter 7.

> Read this portion of Scripture together. You can either read it yourself or ask members of the class to share the responsibility. One way to get through it would be to have a different person read each portion as outlined on page 51 of the Participant's Guide.

Bible Study and Personal Application *(10 minutes)*

> Participant's Guide pages 51, 52, and 53

Before we go on to the video portion of this session, we're going to take a closer look at some of these passages. Turn in your Participant's Guide to page 51. There you have listed for you the eighteen different topics Jesus addresses in the Sermon on the Mount. We're going to break up into smaller groups and read a few of these passages again and then answer the questions found on page 52. There are also two personal application questions found on page 53. We'll have 10 minutes to process this material.

> At this point assign each small group one or two passages so that everyone is studying something different. At the end of 7 minutes encourage the groups to go on to page 53, no matter where they are in their discussion, to allow them to make a personal application of the material.

There is just so much material to cover that we could probably develop a course just on the Sermon on the Mount. Hopefully the last 10 minutes will have encouraged you to study this portion of Scripture more on your own.

Offended? Who, Me?

If you are familiar with the Sermon on the Mount, have you ever considered its message "offensive"?

In our culture, what messages from the church do people often find offensive?

In the church, what kinds of things offend people? What kinds of things offend *you* (honestly!)?

Scripture Reading: The Sermon on the Mount

Matthew 5:13–16	Salt and Light
Matthew 5:17–20	The Law
Matthew 5:21–26	Anger
Matthew 5:27–30	Lust
Matthew 5:32–32	Divorce
Matthew 5:33–36	Vows
Matthew 5:37–42	Retaliation
Matthew 5:43–47	Loving Enemies
Matthew 6:1–4	Giving to the Needy
Matthew 6:5–15	Prayer
Matthew 6:16–18	Fasting
Matthew 6:19–24	Money
Matthew 6: 25–34	Worry
Matthew 7:1–6	Criticizing Others
Matthew 7:7–12	Asking, Seeking, Knocking
Matthew 7:13–14	Way to Heaven
Matthew 7:15–20	Fruit in People's Lives
Matthew 7:21–28	People Who Build Houses on Rock and Sand

Bible Study Questions

Read two or three of the passages found on the preceding page and answer the following questions as they pertain to each passage.

1. What principle does this passage present?

2. Why do you think this message was offensive to those who heard it? Why might it be offensive to those who read it today?

3. What does this passage teach us about God?

4. How does this passage apply in today's settings?

Personal Application

1. It's much easier to study God's laws and tell others to obey them than to put them into practice. How are *you* doing at obeying God?

2. When do you keep God's *rules* but close your eyes to his *intent*?

Video Vignette (approximately 10 minutes)

Participant's Guide page 54

Against all of this discussion we now have the opportunity to hear Philip Yancey's teaching on this subject and to see two different film interpretations of this passage of Scripture. We'll have a short class discussion following the video segment, so you may wish to take notes on page 54 of your Participant's Guide.

View Video Vignette

Philip Yancey—The tough words of Jesus are often watered down. And yet he communicates God's incredible grace.

The Gospel According to St. Matthew—Sermon on the Mount

Son of Man—"Love your enemies"

Class Response (approximately 10 minutes)

Solicit responses from the group to the following questions.

1. The film clips in today's session presented very unusual portrayals of Jesus and his message. What was your initial impression?

2. Do you think that's how Jesus delivered his message? Why or why not?

3. How do you think you would have felt if you had been in the crowd that day?

4. Do you agree with Philip Yancey that many have watered down the message of Jesus? Why or why not?

5. Has there been anything in this session that has been difficult for you?

Summary (1 minute)

Participant's Guide page 55

That concludes our session on Jesus' message. In this session we discussed the different kinds of messages that offend people and how the message of Jesus is "offensive." We also studied the Sermon on the Mount in order to see what it has to say to us today and to ascertain how we can maintain the high ideals of Jesus while still offering his safety net of grace.

In the next session we will discuss Jesus' mission of grace.

Planning Notes

_____

_____

_____

_____

_____

_____

_____

_____

_____

_____

_____

_____

_____

_____

_____

_____

_____

_____

_____

_____

_____

_____

_____

_____

_____

_____

_____

_____

_____

_____

_____

_____

_____

_____

_____

Video Notes
Philip Yancey

The Gospel According to St. Matthew

Son of Man

Summary

In this session we:

- Identified areas where people often are offended.

- Studied the Sermon on the Mount to discover what it has to say to us today.

- Reflected upon the difficulty of maintaining high ideals while still offering a safety net of grace.

Suggested Reading

For more thoughts on this session's topic, read
"Message: A Sermon of Offense,"
chapter 7 of _The Jesus I Never Knew_.

Session Eight:
Mission:
A Revolution of Grace

Before You Lead

Synopsis

As my class in Chicago read the Gospels and watched movies about Jesus' life, we noticed a striking pattern: the more unsavory the characters, the more at ease they seemed to feel around Jesus. In contrast, Jesus got a chilly response from more respectable types. How strange that now the Christian church attracts respectable types who closely resemble the people most suspicious of Jesus on earth. What has happened to reverse the pattern of Jesus' day? Why don't sinners *like* being around Christians and the church today?

"You can know a person by the company he keeps," the proverb goes. Imagine the consternation of people in first-century Palestine who tried to apply that principle to Jesus of Nazareth. Jesus ate with a person known as "the Leper"; twice he allowed a woman to anoint him with oil while at a guest's home; he dined with at least two Pharisees; and he had dinner with at least two tax collectors. Why did Jesus make one group (the sinful) feel so comfortable and the other group (the pious) feel so uncomfortable?

Many first-century Jews preferred John the Baptist's stern message of judgment and wrath to Jesus' message of grace and a banquet spread for all. I can understand this odd preference for the law because of the legalistic environment I grew up in. Grace was slippery, but under law I always knew where I ranked. Similarly, the Jews were operating, in effect, by a religious caste system based on steps toward holiness, and the Pharisees' scrupulosity reinforced the system daily.

Jesus appeared in the midst of this system and had no qualms about socializing with children or sinners or even Samaritans. As Walter Wink noted, Jesus also violated the mores of his time in every single encounter with women recorded in the four gospels. Indeed, for women and other oppressed people, Jesus turned upside down the accepted wisdom of the day. Not only did he reach out to people of all groups, he proclaimed a radically new gospel of grace: to get clean, a person did not have to journey to Jerusalem, offer sacrifices, and undergo purification rituals; all a person had to do was follow Jesus. Jesus moved the emphasis from God's holiness to God's mercy.

In Jesus, God gave us a face, and I can read directly in that face how God feels about people who are poor, sick, or suffering unbelievable injustice. He

96

answered the question of whether God cares. Jesus himself wept in his suffering. I find it strangely comforting that when Jesus faced pain he responded much as I do. He experienced sorrow, fear, abandonment, and something approaching even desperation. Still, he endured because he knew that at the center of the universe lived his Father, a God of love he could trust regardless of how things appeared at the time.

Jesus' response to suffering people and to "nobodies" provides a glimpse into the heart of God. God is not the unmoved Absolute, but rather the Loving One who draws near. God looks on me in all my weakness, I believe, as Jesus looked on the widow standing by her son's corpse, and on Simon the Leper, and on another Simon, Peter, who cursed him yet even so was commissioned to found and lead his church, a community that need always find a place for rejects.

Session Outline

I. Introduction
   Welcome
   Prayer
   Review

II. Warm-Up
   "Outcasts"

III. Content
   Video Vignette
   Class Response
   Bible Study
   Small Group Discussion

IV. Summary
   Review

Materials

No additional materials are needed for this session.

Recommended Reading

"Mission: A Revolution of Grace," chapter 8 of *The Jesus I Never Knew*

Session Eight:
Mission:
A Revolution of Grace

Introduction *(3 minutes)*

Welcome

> Call the group together.
> Welcome the participants to session 8 of *The Jesus I Never Knew* course: "Mission: A Revolution of Grace."

Prayer

Dear Jesus, you came to earth to preach hard words of discipleship and graceful words of acceptance. As we study today your mission of grace, give us the ability to look within ourselves and see where it is we need to display more grace. May the words we speak be filled with understanding and compassion. Give us the ability to listen to the ideas of others rather than impatiently waiting to share our own. Amen.

Review

> Participant's Guide page 57

In the last session we studied the Sermon on the Mount and looked at the many ways Jesus offended people and called for discipleship. In this session we're going to look carefully at Jesus' mission of grace. We'll begin by talking a little bit about those who were considered outcasts in Jesus' day and in our society today and then we'll go to Philip Yancey, the film clips, and the Bible to identify how Jesus communicated God's grace. Finally, we'll consider how we can communicate mercy toward sinners and encourage genuine worship of Jesus at the same time.

Planning Notes

- WELCOME
  - THANK YOU TO LAURALEE
    FOR LEADING LAST WEEK
  - WELCOME BACK TO SCOTT
    AND FOR ALL THE TECHNICAL
    HELP WE GOT TO STAY CONNECTED
  - PRAYERS FOR SUSAN

- LET US OPEN WITH A PRAYER

- REVIEW
  - TO KEEP US THINKING
    THROUGH THIS STUDY AS
    A FLOW/CONTINUUM
    - OUR PERCEPTIONS OF JESUS
    - HIS BIRTH
    - HIS CULTURAL/CONTEXTUAL
      FIT AS A JEW
    - HIS TEMPTATIONS
    - HIS PHYSICAL LOOKS AND HIS MSG
    - THE BEATITUDES (BLESSINGS)
    - THE SERMON ON THE MOUNT

- TODAY WE EXPLORE THE "ATTRACTION" (MY WORD)
  OF JESUS IN THE FIRST CENTURY AND
  TODAY... WHO DOES HE CALL/ATTRACT AND
  WHO DOES HE INTIMIDATE... THEN AND NOW

  - WE'LL THINK ABOUT THESE QUESTIONS
    AND WE'LL TALK ABOUT OUR CHURCH

Session Eight:
Mission: A Revolution of Grace

Questions To Consider

- Who are the "outcasts" of society?

- How did Jesus communicate God's grace?

- How does/can *our* church communicate mercy toward sinners *and* encourage genuine worship of Jesus?

A CLOSER LOOK @...

57

Warm-Up (5 minutes)

"Outcasts"

Participant's Guide page 58

Turn to page 58 in your Participant's Guide. Jesus was a man who associated with all kinds of people. One of the religious leaders' greatest sources of consternation with him was the fact that he so often spent time with the people in their society who were misfits and outcasts.

Solicit responses from the group to the following questions.

◆ Can you think of individuals or groups who are considered "outcasts" in the Bible?

Possible Answers: People with leprosy, the poor, Gentiles or people from other races, prostitutes, tax collectors, those with illnesses or disabilities. Also, men in Jewish culture often looked down upon women (although they were not considered outcasts), and Jewish religious leaders often looked down upon the common person.

◆ Which individuals or groups are sometimes considered "outcasts" in our world today?

Possible Answers: The homeless, the destitute, those with AIDS, the poor, those with disabilities, illegal immigrants, prisoners

Content (35 minutes)

Video Vignette (approximately 10 minutes)

Participant's Guide page 59

Philip Yancey has a few interesting observations about Jesus' grace. Let's view today's video segment, which also contains a confrontation involving religious leaders and an adulteress, along with a potrayal of Jesus telling the story of the Prodigal Son.

View Video Vignette
Philip Yancey—In Jesus' day the ungodly were attracted to Jesus and the "righteous" were made uncomfortable.
Gospel Road—Stoning the adulteress
Jesus of Nazareth—Prodigal Son

Planning Notes

(5-10)

- TURN TO PG 58
  - INDIVIDUALLY CONSIDER THESE QUESTIONS
  - SOLICIT RESPONSES / COMMENTS AFTER
    5 MINUTES

- VIDEOS (TURN THE PAGE)

"Outcasts"

Can you think of individuals or groups who are considered "outcasts" in the Bible?

- LEPERS, PROSTITUTES, TAX COLLECTORS > BY SOCIETY

- PHARISEES, HYPOCRITES > DESPISED BY JESUS

Which individuals or groups are sometimes considered "outcasts" in our world today?

- POOR / WELFARE, "UNBEAUTIFUL" PEOPLE > BY SOCIETY
  FOREIGNERS / ILLEGAL ALIENS ...

- SINNERS, SELFISH / NON-GIVERS > MADE TO BE
  LESS DEVOUT?   UNCOMFORTABLE
       (OR SELF-IMPOSED)
       BY THE CHURCH

- MUSLIMS? OTHER RACES?

Video Notes
Philip Yancey

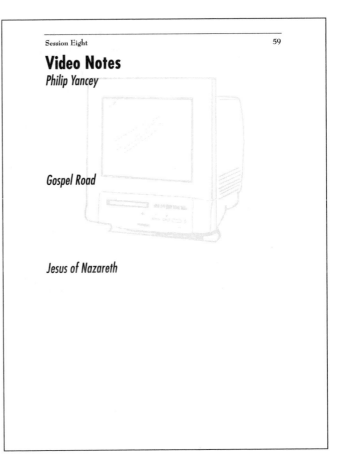

Gospel Road

Jesus of Nazareth

Class Response *(5 minutes)*

Solicit responses from the group to the following questions.

1. Philip Yancey talked about the way the ungodly were attracted to Jesus while the "righteous" were uncomfortable with him. He also believes that today the church has reversed that trend. Do you think this is an accurate observation? Why or why not?

2. What was your initial response to the scene from *The Gospel Road?* What about the Prodigal Son story in *Jesus of Nazareth?*

3. How can the church show concern about moral issues while demonstrating a gracious spirit toward immoral people?

Bible Study and Small Group Discussion *(20 minutes)*

Participant's Guide pages 60 and 61

This study will be done in small groups with the groups reporting back to the larger group in the last 5 minutes.

Turn to page 60 in your Participant's Guide. The Scripture passage here is only one example of the way Jesus interacted with those whom others would never associate with publicly. However, the principles we can learn from this passage will give us a great deal to think about. After briefly discussing the information on page 60, go on to page 61. Don't use this as an assignment of a formal evaluation of our church, but rather as a reflective discussion on how we might corporately respond to Jesus' message of grace.

Give the groups 15 minutes to process the material. Let them know when they have 10 minutes remaining and should consider moving on to page 61. Then let them know again when they have 1 minute left so that they can decide which one idea they would like to share with the rest of the class.

Have one person from each small group share their key idea with the larger group.

Planning Notes

-10
• VIDEO

① READ THE QUESTION ON LH PG   (✱)

②/③ WHAT WAS YOUR RESPONSE TO THESE?

④ IS THERE A DILEMMA OR A CONFLICT IN
MSG REGARDING MORALITY IN OUR CHURCH?
DO WE COMPROMISE OUR EMPHASIS ON MORAL
BEHAVIOR WITH OUR GRACIOUS SPIRIT / OUR
FORGIVENESS OF IMMORAL PEOPLE?

⑩ • VOLUNTEER TO READ MATTHEW 9: 9-13...
THEN ASK SOMEONE TO READ PG 60

— DISCUSS QUESTION ON PG 60

⑩
...NOW TURN TO PG 61... BREAK INTO 2 GROUPS (GRP 1 = 61, GRP 2 = 62, BOTH GRPS = Q3)

Video Notes

Ⓐ **Philip Yancey**
THE BALANCE HAS SHIFTED.- YOU SEE FAR MORE "WEALTHY"
IN CHURCH THAN HOMELESS... A FUNCTION OF LOCATION
(I.E., PG/RB = UPPER MIDDLE CLASS). BUT ALSO POSSIBLY
A SENSE OF "WANTING GOD ON MY SIDE"?

Gospel Road

Jesus of Nazareth

Bible Study

Read Matthew 9:9–13—"Jesus Eats with Sinners at a Tax Collector's House"

In Jesus' day tax collectors collected taxes on a commission basis, pocketing whatever profits they could extort from the locals. Most Jews viewed them as traitors serving the Roman empire. The words tax collector were synonymous with robber, brigand, murderer, and reprobate. Jewish courts considered a tax collector's evidence as invalid, and his money could not be accepted as alms for the poor or used in exchange since it had been acquired by such despicable means.

It seems that the more unsavory the characters, the more at ease they seemed to feel around Jesus. In contrast, Jesus got a chilly response from more respectable types. How strange that now the Christian church attracts respectable types who closely resemble the people most suspicious of Jesus on earth. What has happened to reverse the pattern of Jesus' day? Why don't sinners like being around Christians and the church today?

(✱) On a scale of 1 to 10, how is our church doing in attracting sinners to our fellowship?

— SCALE?
— WHAT IS A SINNER?

Let's consider that topic in greater detail. Go to the next page and discuss the questions there. Choose one person from your group to highlight one or two points of your discussion to be shared with the entire class.

— IS IT A GOAL TO ATTRACT SINNERS?

Small Group Discussion

1. How does/can our church communicate mercy toward sinners?

Preaching — OUTSIDE OF CHURCH WALLS (WEBSITES/PODCAST

Worship service format — VARIED

Programs — TRADITIONAL AND "EDGY" (CONTEMPORARY FORMAT AND MSG... TALK TO THE SINS OF TODAY.. DIVORCE,

Community service — OUTREACH MINISTRY

2. How does/can our church encourage genuine worship of Jesus?

Preaching   ADULTERY, THEFT, SELFISH ENTITLEMENT)

Worship service format

Lay people participating in worship — YES

Music

Sunday school

Small groups

Other programs

3. What can we/I do to help our church in this process?

— REACH/EXTEND ONESELF (NOT TEACHING)

Summary *(1 minute)*

Participant's Guide page 62

That concludes our session on Jesus' mission of grace. In this session we identified some of the individuals and groups who were considered "outcasts" in Jesus' day as well as in our own. We also studied the way Jesus communicated grace and identified some of the ways our church does and can communicate mercy toward sinners as well as encourage genuine worship of Jesus.

In the next session we will study another important aspect of Jesus' ministry—his miracles.

Planning Notes

> SOLICIT PRAYER/PRAISE
> REQUESTS (JEFF)

• CLOSING PRAYER (VOLUNTEER)

5/25 PRAYERS

- SCOTT'S OUTREACH.. FOR AIDS
  SAFETY..
SUSIE CONNOR (11) – LYMPHOMA/LEUKEMIA
MIKE ALEX .. LOST HIS JOB
- DAVE = JOANN NEEDS A CAR
        DAVE NEEDS A CAR + A PLACE TO
        STAY BY 31 MAY
        UNSPOKEN PRAYERS
        THANKFUL FOR SUCCESS
        OF PRAISE/FRIENDS
- LAURALEE: ALLERGIES WHILE
        VISITING DAUGHTER

SCOTT = TRACY (FRIEND OF FLYNNS)
        HAS PANCREATITIS

DAVE: JEN HAS PANCREATITIS

Summary

In this session we:

• Identified the "outcasts" in the Bible and in our society.

• Studied the way in which Jesus communicated grace.

• Identified ways in which our church does and can communicate mercy toward sinners *and* encourage genuine worship of Jesus.

Suggested Reading

For more thoughts on this session's topic, read "Mission: A Revolution of Grace," chapter 8 of *The Jesus I Never Knew*.

Session Nine:
Miracles: Snapshots of the Supernatural

Before You Lead

Synopsis

As I was growing up, I envisioned Jesus as the Great Magician, and his miracles as magic. As I now reflect on his life, miracles play a less prominent role than I had imagined. Jesus' miracles generated excitement but not always faith. Why did he perform so few miracles? Why any at all? Why these particular miracles?

Miracles of healing captured the most attention. Jesus overturned common notions about how God views sick and disabled people. He denied that a man's blindness came from any sin, just as he dismissed the common opinion that tragedies happen to those who deserve them (see Luke 13:1–5). Jesus wanted the sick to know they are especially loved, not cursed, by God.

The only miracle that appears in all four gospels is the feeding of the five thousand, taking place on the grassy hills near the shores of Galilee. Here, after being miraculously fed in the middle of nowhere, the crowd intends to seize Jesus by force and crown him king. But he was not that kind of Messiah. His was a hard message of obedience and sacrifice, not a sideshow for gawkers and sensation seekers.

As I now read the accounts of selected miracles from Jesus' time, I find in them a very different message. In no event did the miracles bowl people over and steamroller them into belief. Otherwise there would be no room for faith. I now see miracles as signs rather than magic. Jesus' miracles did little to solve the problem of pain on this planet, yet through them Jesus showed that it was in his nature to counteract the effects of the fallen world during his time on earth. Miracles are early glimpses of the restoration of the universe.

As I have gone through all the Gospel accounts of miracles, I have come up with the following observations. These do not constitute a "philosophy of miracles" by any means. They are simply my personal observations.

- The Gospels record about three dozen incidents of miracles, some of which were group healings. Although impressive, these miracles affected a relatively small number of people, in one small corner of the world. Jesus performed no miracles of healing for the Chinese, for example, or Europeans. His miracles tended to be quite selective.

- Jesus resisted performing miracles "on demand" to prove himself, even when he had good opportunity to do so (before Herod, with Satan in the wilderness, to impress doubters who were demanding a sign).

- Jesus often hushed up his miracles, ordering people to "tell no one" about them. He seemed wary of the kind of faith miracles can produce: an attraction for the spectacular, rather than the kind of lifelong commitment he was after.

- Jesus' miracles sometimes created distance, not intimacy. For example, when Jesus calmed the storm, the disciples in the boat with him drew back, terrified.

- People in Jesus' day found it no easier to believe in miracles than do people in our modern skeptical age. For example, the Pharisees in John 9 worked hard to disprove the blind man's story. Similarly, they responded to Lazarus's resurrection by seeking another opportunity to kill him. Most astonishing, the Roman soldiers who actually witnessed the greatest miracle, the resurrection of Christ, experienced no great change of heart—instead, they changed their story in return for a payoff.

- Most miracles of healing came about because of Jesus' compassion, often because the sight of a suffering person moved him. Several times he fled from crowds who were pressing around him, demanding even more miracles.

- Spiritual miracles tended to impress Jesus more than physical ones. Remarkable or unusual faith impressed him most. When he healed a paralyzed man who was lowered to him through a roof, Jesus asked, "Which is easier: to say to the paralytic, 'Your sins are forgiven,' or to say, 'Get up, take your mat and walk'?" (Mark 2:9). Jesus' entire ministry provides an answer. Physical healing was far easier, without question. Jesus knew that spiritual disease has a more devastating effect than any mere physical ailment. Why is it, I wonder, that many ministries are founded that focus on physical miracles, but I know of few organized to combat sins like pride or greed?

- Jesus also performed miracles to establish his credentials—so that when he declared who he was, he would have some evidence to back up the claim. "Even though you do not believe me, believe the miracles, that you may know and understand that the Father is in me, and I in the Father" (John 10:38).

- Though they did not solve all problems on earth, Jesus' miracles were a sign of how the world should be and someday will be. They were, in fact, a preview of the future.

- Jesus performed no miracles for the purposes of fund-raising, fame, or self-protection. Unlike other miracle workers, he did not try to encourage mystery or wonder or appeal to a sense of magic. And denying his disciples' requests, he never performed miracles of retaliation.

Session Outline

I. Introduction
   Welcome
   Prayer
   Review

II. Warm-Up
   Miracles

III. Content
   Video Vignette
   Group Response
   Bible Study

IV. Summary

Materials

No additional materials are needed for this session.

Recommended Reading

"Miracles: Snapshots of the Supernatural," chapter 9 of *The Jesus I Never Knew*

Session Nine:
Miracles: Snapshots of the Supernatural

Introduction *(3 Minutes)*

Welcome

> Call the group together.
> Welcome the participants to session 9 of *The Jesus I Never Knew* course: "Miracles: Snapshots of the Supernatural."

Prayer

Dear Jesus, we are so grateful for the way you reveal yourself to us. As we study your miracles today, give us new insight into who you are and how much you care for us all. Help us to see with new eyes how you cared for those you interacted with while you were on earth. And above all, help us to stay true to you and your teachings in all that we discuss today. Amen.

Review

In the last session we discussed God's grace as revealed in the life of Jesus. We talked about the "outcasts" in Jesus' life as well as in our own. We also tried to identify ways in which we, as individuals and corporately as our church, can communicate God's mercy toward sinners and encourage genuine worship of Christ.

> Participant's Guide page 63

In this session we will focus our attention on the miracles of Jesus. We'll begin by reflecting on our impressions of Jesus when we were children and then study some of the miracles Jesus did. The video segment today has some interesting and challenging material in it.

Planning Notes

Session Nine:
Miracles: Snapshots of the Supernatural

Questions To Consider

- What was your view of miracles as you were growing up?

- What were some of the miracles of Jesus, and why did he do them?

- What lessons from the miracles of Jesus can we apply today?

63

Warm-Up *(5–10 minutes)*

Miracles

> Participant's Guide page 64

Turn to page 64 in your Participant's Guide. We've tried to begin each one of our sessions by identifying our past and existing views on a specific topic. This session is about Jesus' miracles.

> Ask the questions found on page 64 and solicit responses from the group for each one.

◆ What was your view of miracles as you were growing up?

> Possible Answers: Magic; a vending machine, with prayer as the coin; proof that Jesus was God; the Devil's power; exaggerated stories; the answer to human pain; Jesus' opportunity to show he cared.

◆ List some of the miracles of Jesus that you recall.

> Possible Answers: The wedding at Cana; healing the blind man; healing the person with leprosy; healing Jairus' daughter; feeding the 5,000; walking on the water; raising Lazarus

◆ Take a look at two or three of your responses. Why did Jesus do them? What was his motivation?

> As the leader, choose the ones you wish to discuss.

Let's continue to think about these ideas as we view the video segment.

Content *(30–35 minutes)*

Video Vignette *(approximately 10 minutes)*

> Participant's Guide page 65

> View Video Vignette
> *Jesus*—Healing of the blind man
> *Gospel Road*—Different scenes with Jesus
> *Philip Yancey*—His personal observations about miracles

Planning Notes

_____
_____
_____
_____
_____
_____
_____
_____
_____
_____
_____
_____
_____
_____
_____
_____
_____
_____
_____
_____
_____
_____
_____
_____
_____
_____
_____
_____
_____
_____
_____
_____

Miracles

What was your view of miracles as you were growing up?

List some of the miracles of Jesus that you recall.

Take a look at two or three of your responses. Why did Jesus do them? What was his motivation?

Video Notes
Jesus

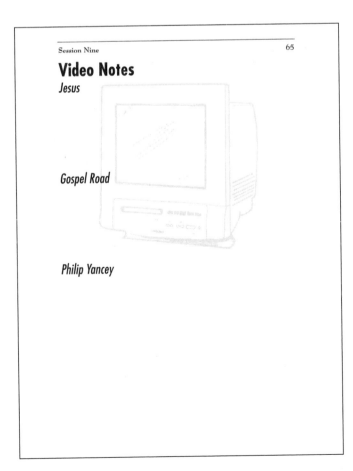

Gospel Road

Philip Yancey

Class Response *(5 minutes)*

> Solicit answers from the group for the following questions.

1. When Jesus performed healings, do you think it was anything like the portrayals in the film clips? Why or why not?

2. What was the most thought-provoking observation from Philip Yancey?

3. Do you believe Jesus still performs miracles in the world today? Why or why not?

Bible Study *(15–20 minutes)*

> Participant's Guide pages 66 and 67

> This study will be done in small groups with the groups reporting back to the larger group in the last 5 minutes. Assign each group a different miracle and passage of Scripture.

Let's break into groups of four and study a little more carefully several of Jesus' miracles. Turn to pages 66 and 67 in your Participant's Guide and take 10 minutes to read one of the assigned Scripture passages and work through these questions. Choose one person in your group to report back to the whole class on one key idea you discussed.

> Give the groups 10–15 minutes to process the material. Let them know when they have 1 minute remaining.

> Have one person from each small group share their key idea with the larger group.

Planning Notes

_____

_____

_____

_____

_____

_____

_____

_____

_____

_____

_____

_____

_____

_____

_____

_____

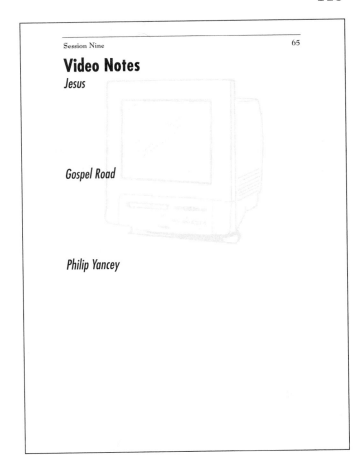

Video Notes
Jesus

Gospel Road

Philip Yancey

Bible Study

Read one of the following passages describing a miracle that Jesus performed and then answer the questions, choosing one key idea to share with the whole group.

John 2:1–11	Wine at the wedding feast of Cana
Matthew 14:15–21	Feeding of the 5,000
Matthew 9:20–22	Healing of the bleeding woman
Mark 9:14–29	Healing of the boy with an evil spirit
Matthew 8:28–34	Demons sent into the pigs
Luke 17:11–19	Healing of the ten with leprosy

1. What does this passage tell you about Jesus?

2. What kind of impact did this miracle have on those around the situation at the time: family, friends, the crowd, the religious leaders? Is there any indication that people acknowledged Jesus as the Messiah because of this miracle? Or is there any indication that people's faith was increased?

---

3. Why do you think Jesus chose to perform this particular miracle?

4. Does Jesus still work miracles of this sort in similar situations? What is usually the outcome if this type of miracle does occur? What *might* be the outcome if it did?

5. What have you learned in this session that has been new for you?

Summary *(1 minute)*

Participant's Guide page 68

In this session we discussed our various impressions of miracles when we were children, identified some of the miracles of Jesus, and tried to ascertain his motivation for doing them. We also attempted to apply some of the lessons Jesus taught through his miracles to our own lives.

Philip Yancey makes the point in his book that, although Jesus had all the supernatural powers at his command, he showed ambivalence toward miracles. They attracted crowds and applause, yes, but they rarely encouraged repentance and long-term faith. Jesus was bringing a hard message of obedience and sacrifice, not a sideshow for gawkers and sensation-seekers.

In our next session we will study Jesus' death including the events preceding it.

Planning Notes

Summary

In this session we:

- Discussed our various impressions of miracles when we were children.

- Identified some of the miracles of Jesus and tried to ascertain his motivation for doing them.

- Applied some of the lessons Jesus taught through his miracles to our own lives.

Suggested Reading

For more thoughts on this session's topic, read
"Miracles: Snapshots of the Supernatural,"
chapter 9 of *The Jesus I Never Knew*.

Session Ten:
Death: The Final Week

Before You Lead

Synopsis

The church I grew up in skipped past the events of Holy Week in a rush to hear the cymbal sounds of Easter. We never held a service on Good Friday. We celebrated the Lord's Supper only once per quarter. Yet the Gospels devote nearly a third of their length to the climactic last week of Jesus' life. Matthew, Mark, Luke, and John saw death as the central mystery of Jesus.

How can we who know the outcome in advance ever recapture the dire end-of-the-world feeling that descended upon Jesus' followers? I will merely record what stands out to me as I review the Passion story one more time.

Triumphal Entry. An adoring crowd makes up the ragtag procession: the lame, the blind, the children, the peasants from Galilee and Bethany. I imagine a Roman soldier galloping up to check on the disturbance. He spies a forlorn figure, weeping, riding on no stallion or chariot but on the back of a baby donkey, a borrowed coat draped across the animal's backbone serving as his saddle. Jesus wept as he viewed the city that could so easily turn on him.

The Last Supper. In Jesus' day, footwashing was considered so degrading that a master could not require it of a Jewish slave. In one act on an evening shortly before his death, however, Jesus symbolically overturned the whole social order. He washed the feet of his disciples. Hardly comprehending what was happening, they were almost horrified by his behavior. This act became one of three things Jesus asked his followers to do to remember him, with baptism and celebrating the Lord's Supper being the others. Following his example of footwashing was not easy for Jesus' disciples and has not become any easier in two thousand years.

Betrayal. As I read the Gospel accounts, it is Judas's ordinariness, not his villainy, that stands out. The Gospels contain no hint that Judas had been a "mole" infiltrating the inner circle to plan his treachery. Judas was not the first or the last ordinary person to betray Jesus. To Shusaku Endo, the most powerful message of Jesus was his unquenchable love even for—especially for—people who betrayed him. When Judas led a lynch mob into the garden, Jesus addressed him as "friend." The other disciples deserted Jesus but still he loved them. His nation had him executed, yet while stretched out naked in the posture of ultimate disgrace, Jesus roused himself for the cry, "Father, forgive them . . . "

I know of no more poignant contrast between two human destinies than that of Peter and Judas. Peter denied knowing Jesus three times on the eve of Jesus' death. Judas betrayed Jesus for thirty silver coins. Judas, remorseful but apparently unrepentant, took his own life and went down as the greatest traitor in history. He died unwilling to receive what Jesus had come to offer him. Peter, humiliated but still open to Jesus' message of grace and forgiveness, went on to lead a revival in Jerusalem and did not stop until he had reached Rome.

Gethsemane. By instinct, we humans want someone by our side in any great moment of crisis. I detect in the Gospels' account of Gethsemane a profound depth of loneliness that Jesus had never before encountered. Jesus was by no means powerless. But here he relived Satan's temptation in the desert. Either time he could have solved the problem of evil by force, with a quick stab of the Accuser in the desert or a fierce battle in the garden. All this lay within Jesus' power if he merely said the word. Yet as John Howard Yoder reminds us, the "cup" that now seemed so terrifying was the very reason Jesus had come to earth.

The trials. Unlike a defendant in today's courtroom dramas, Jesus faced as many as six interrogations in the span of less than twenty-four hours, some conducted by the Jews and some by the Romans. In the end, an exasperated governor pronounced the harshest verdict permitted under Roman law. As I read the trial transcripts, Jesus' defenselessness stands out. Not a single witness rose to his defense. No leader had the nerve to speak out against injustice. Not even Jesus tried to defend himself. To the priests and the pious, Jesus represented a threat to the Law, the sacrificial system, the temple, and the many distinctions between clean and unclean. His claims about himself were too much. How could they be true? Jesus looked to be the least Messiah-like figure in all of Israel. Yet weak, rejected, doomed, utterly alone, only now does Jesus think it safe to reveal himself and accept the title "Christ," or Messiah.

Calvary. Even after watching scores of moves on the subject and reading the Gospels over and over, I still cannot fathom the indignity, the shame, endured by God's Son on earth, stripped naked, flogged, spat on, struck in the face, garlanded with thorns. Nothing—nothing—in history compares to the self-restraint shown that dark Friday in Jerusalem. With every lash of the whip, every fibrous crunch of fist against flesh, Jesus must have mentally replayed the temptation in the wilderness and in Gethsemane. Legions of angels awaited his command. One word and the ordeal would end. No theologian can adequately explain the nature of what took place within the Trinity on that day at Calvary. All we have is a cry from a child who felt abandoned: "My God, my God, why have you forsaken me?" (Matt. 27:46).

In a sense, the paired thieves crucified on either side of Jesus present the choice that all history has had to decide about the cross. Do we look at Jesus' powerlessness as an example of God's impotence or as proof of God's love? The cross redefines God as one who was willing to relinquish power for the sake of love. Power, no matter how well-intentioned, tends to cause suffering. Love, being vulnerable, absorbs it. In a point of convergence on a hill called Calvary, God renounced the one for the sake of the other.

Session Outline

I. Introduction
   Welcome
   Prayer
   Review

II. Warm-Up
   Celebrating Holy Week

III. Content
   Video Vignette
   Class Response
   Bible Study
   Personal Reflection

IV. Summary

Materials

No additional materials are needed for this session.

Recommended Reading

"Death: The Final Week," chapter 10 of *The Jesus I Never Knew*

Session Ten:
Death:
The Final Week

Introduction *(3 minutes)*

Welcome

> Call the group together.
> Welcome the participants to session 10 of *The Jesus I Never Knew* course: "Death: The Final Week."

Prayer

Heavenly Father, it is so difficult for us to understand your Son's life, and even more difficult for us to comprehend his death. For many of us Easter has become just another religious holiday. Help us today to read the Scriptures as if for the first time, to grasp the incredible truth that you loved us so much your Son was willing to die a criminal's death for us. Give us a new appreciation for what that means today. In Jesus' name, we come before you. Amen.

Review

In the last session we studied the miracles of Jesus and tried not only to understand why he did them, but also to apply some of the lessons to our own lives. In this session we will look at the culmination of Jesus' life—through the lens of his final week on earth.

> Participant's Guide page 69

The material today will help us to think about Holy Week—the week before Easter, including Jesus' crucifixion. Philip Yancey will share with us his ideas on why the death of Jesus is a critical event and we'll take an in-depth look at three events leading to Jesus' death: the Triumphal Entry, the Last Supper and Jesus' trial. We'll also take a look at the Crucifixion and consider our individual responses to Jesus' death.

Session Ten:
Death:
The Final Week

Questions To Consider

- In what ways do we commemorate Holy Week, the week *before* Easter?

- Why is the death of Jesus such a critical event?

- What do we learn about Jesus in each of the events leading up to and including his death: the Triumphal Entry, the Last Supper, his trial, and his crucifixion?

- What is my *personal* response to the death of Jesus Christ?

Warm-Up *(5 minutes)*

Celebrating Holy Week

> Participant's Guide page 70

Turn to page 70 in your Participant's Guide. As we begin our discussion of Holy Week, let's identify some of our own remembrances of some of the significant events leading up to the Crucifixion.

> Solicit responses from the group to the following two questions.

❖ How does our church celebrate Holy Week, the week before Easter?

❖ What other activities have you experienced to commemorate Holy Week?

> Possible Answers: Ash Wednesday, Communion, Maundy Thursday service, Seder meal, foot washing service, Good Friday service, fasting

All of these experiences help us to remember Jesus' death.

Content *(35 minutes)*

Video Vignette (approximately 10 minutes)

> Participant's Guide page 71

In this session, Philip Yancey will lead in to the film clip with an explanation of why the Gospels focus so much on Jesus' death rather than his resurrection. You may wish to take notes on page 71 of your Participant's Guide.

> View Video Vignette
> *Philip Yancey*—Why the Gospels focus so much on Jesus' death, rather than his resurrection
> *Witnesses*—Thomas recalling Jesus' life

Planning Notes

_____
_____
_____
_____
_____
_____
_____
_____
_____
_____
_____
_____
_____
_____
_____
_____
_____
_____
_____
_____
_____
_____
_____
_____
_____
_____
_____
_____
_____
_____
_____
_____
_____
_____
_____
_____
_____
_____

---

70   The Jesus I Never Knew Participant's Guide

Celebrating Holy Week

How does our church celebrate Holy Week, the week before Easter?

What other activities have you experienced to commemorate Holy Week?

Session Ten   71

Video Notes
Philip Yancey

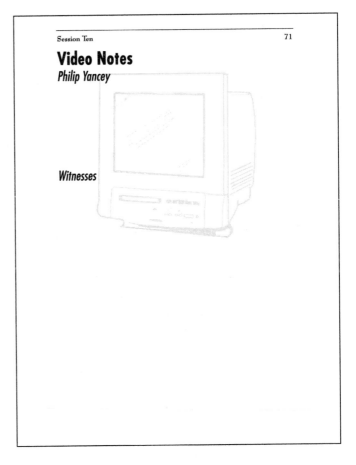

Witnesses

Class Response (5 minutes)

Solicit responses from the group to the following questions.

1. Were you disappointed that we didn't see a re-enactment of one of the Holy Week events? Have you ever seen the Crucifixion portrayed movingly, such as in a Passion play or movie?

2. How realistic do you think the Thomas portrayal was from the *Witnesses* film?

3. Do you agree or disagree with Philip Yancey's observations about Jesus' death?

Bible Study (15 minutes)

Participant's Guide pages 72, 73, 74, and 75

For this session, divide your class into four groups—even if the groups only have two people in them. If your class has more than sixty participants, you may wish to divide the groups into smaller groups of ten and have several groups work on the same passage. Allow the groups 10 minutes to work through their specific page, and then have one person from each group share their answer to question #2.

We're going to break into four small groups and have each group take a different event in Holy Week: The Triumphal Entry, the Last Supper, Jesus' trial, and the Crucifixion. You'll have 10 minutes to work through your questions and then we'll have one person from each group share your group's response to question #2.

Give the groups 10 minutes to work. Let them know when they have 1 minute remaining.

Have the groups share their ideas in the order the events are listed in the Participant's Guide: The Triumphal Entry, the Last Supper, Jesus' trial, and the Crucifixion.

Bible Study
The Triumphal Entry

Read Luke 19: 28–44

1. What is happening in this passage?

2. Why is this event significant?

3. Is this event the same or different from some of Jesus' other interactions with the crowds at different times in his ministry? Explain.

4. How would you have responded to this event had you been in the crowd that day? If you were one of Jesus' disciples? If you were one of the religious rulers?

Bible Study
The Last Supper

Read Matthew 26:26–29

1. What is happening in this passage?

2. Why is this event significant?

3. Is this event the same or different from some of Jesus' other interactions with his disciples at different times in his ministry? Explain.

4. How would you have felt if you had been one of the disciples that day?

Bible Study
Jesus on Trial

Matthew 26:57–27:2, 11–31

1. What is happening in this passage?

2. Why is this event significant?

3. As Jesus' stands before the authorities, is his behavior the same or different from other times in his ministry? Explain.

4. How would you have responded to this event had you been in the crowd that day? If you were one of Jesus' disciples? If you were one of the religious rulers?

Bible Study
The Crucifixion

Read Matthew 27:31–56

1. What is happening in this passage?

2. Why is this event significant?

3. How would you have felt if you had been in the crowd that day? If you were one of Jesus' disciples? If you were one of the religious rulers? If you were visiting the city just for the day?

4. What does the Crucifixion teach us about God?

Personal Reflection (5 minutes)

Participant's Guide page 76

To close this session we're going to take 5 minutes to answer the Personal Reflection questions found on page 76 of your Participant's Guide. Ultimately each one of us must respond to Jesus' death personally.

Give the participants 5 minutes to work. Let them know when they have 1 minute remaining.

Summary (1 minute)

Participant's Guide page 77

As Philip Yancey has pointed out in his book, there is no way we who know the outcome in advance can ever recapture the dire end-of-the-world feeling that descended upon Jesus' followers when he died on the cross. Over the centuries, the story has grown so familiar that we cannot comprehend, much less recreate, the impact of that final week on those who lived through it.

However, despite the shame and sadness of it all, somehow what took place on a hill called Calvary has become arguably the most important fact of Jesus' life—for the writers of the Gospels and Epistles, for the church, and, as far as we can speculate on such matters, for God as well.

Of course, the logical progression beyond this session is to study Jesus' resurrection, which we will do in our next session.

Planning Notes

_____

_____

_____

_____

_____

_____

_____

_____

_____

_____

_____

_____

_____

_____

_____

_____

_____

_____

_____

_____

_____

_____

_____

_____

_____

_____

_____

_____

_____

_____

_____

_____

_____

_____

_____

_____

Personal Reflection

1. Having been through this session, how has my understanding grown regarding Jesus' final week on earth?

2. What can/will I do during the next Lenten period to observe Holy Week in a meaningful way?

3. Do I truly believe that Jesus died for *me*? How is this belief reflected in my everyday life?

Summary

In this session we:

- Reflected on the various ways we commemorate Holy Week.

- Identified why the death of Jesus is such a critical event.

- Discovered some important truths regarding the events leading up to and including Jesus' death: the Triumphal Entry, the Last Supper, his trial, and the Crucifixion.

- Considered our response to the death of Christ.

> ### Suggested Reading
> For more thoughts on this session's topic, read
> "Death: The Final Week,"
> chapter 10 of *The Jesus I Never Knew*.

Session Eleven:
Resurrection: A Morning Beyond Belief

Before You Lead

Synopsis

As a child, when my kitten was killed by a dog, I learned the meaning of the word *irreversible*. Not so long ago, when three of my friends died in quick succession, the ugly word *irreversible* came flooding back. As I spoke at one of the funerals, I asked what would happen if our friend rose and appeared in the parking lot, alive again. That image gave me a hint of what Jesus' disciples felt on the first Easter.

The Gospels present the resurrection of Jesus as a shocking intrusion that no one was expecting, least of all Jesus' timorous disciples. Yet in their joy the disciples still took some convincing. We who read the Gospels from the other side of Easter, who have the day printed on our calendars, forget how hard it was for the disciples to believe. Jesus didn't make glamorous appearances but rather showed up in the most ordinary circumstances. He could always prove his identity, yet often the disciples failed to recognize him right away. Painstakingly he would condescend to meet the level of their skepticism, eating fish, inviting Thomas to finger his scars, instructing Peter in front of six friends.

That Jesus succeeded in changing a snuffling band of unreliable followers into fearless evangelists, that eleven men who had deserted him at death now went to martyrs' graves, avowing their faith in a resurrected Christ, that these few witnesses managed to set loose a force that would overcome violent opposition first in Jerusalem and then in Rome—this remarkable sequence of transformation offers the most convincing evidence for the Resurrection.

Although God allows death, I believe that he is not satisfied with such a blighted planet. Divine love will find a way to overcome. Because of Easter, I can hope that the tears we shed, the blows we receive, the emotional pain, the heartache over lost friends and loved ones, all these will become memories, like Jesus' scars. Scars never completely go away, but neither do they hurt any longer. We will have re-created bodies, a re-created heaven and earth. We will have a new start, an Easter start.

Session Outline

 I. Introduction
  Welcome
  Prayer
  Review

 II. Warm-Up
  Easter!

 III. Content
  Bible Reading
  Video Vignette
  Class Response
  Small Group Discussion

 IV. Summary

Materials

If possible, a recording of Sandi Patty's, "Was It a Morning Like This?" to be used as part of the warm-up exercise. You will also need whatever type of equipment necessary for playing the recording (tape player, CD player, cords, etc.).

Recommended Reading

"Resurrection: A Morning Beyond Belief," chapter 11 of *The Jesus I Never Knew*

Session Eleven:
Resurrection: A Morning Beyond Belief

Introduction *(3 minutes)*

Welcome

> Call the group together.
> Welcome the participants to session 11 of *The Jesus I Never Knew* course: "Resurrection: A Morning Beyond Belief."

Prayer

Heavenly Father, what was it really like to experience that first Easter morning? We sense true joy, yet also fear and confusion among those closest to Jesus. What a mixture of emotions on a day we now celebrate with so much enthusiasm. As we look at the morning again today through a different set of lenses, give us a new appreciation and understanding of what Jesus Christ's resurrection represents. Amen.

Review

At the conclusion of our last session, we left Jesus in the grave. Throughout our time together we discussed the different ways we commemorate Holy Week and studied the various events leading up to his crucifixion. We ended that session by considering our personal responses to the death of Jesus.

> Participant's Guide page 79

In this session we are going to focus on the Resurrection. We'll take a look at how we celebrate Easter today and then go back and study what *really* happened on the first Easter. Finally we'll talk about some of the doubts we may have surrounding Jesus' resurrection.

Planning Notes

- WELCOME
  - MISSED THE LAST TWO WEEKS AND WISH I'D BEEN HOME
  -

- OPENING PRAYER

- REVIEW
  - ⁴⁾WE STARTED WITH OUR PERCEPTIONS OF JESUS
  - ⁵⁾HAVE PROGRESSED IN STUDY FM HIS BIRTH,³⁾TO HIS JEWISHNESS⁴⁾TO HIS TEMPTATIONS,⁵⁾TO HIS ADULT APPEARANCE, HIS MESSAGE AND THE BEATITUDES AS WELL AS ⁷⁾HIS SERMON ON THE MOUNT. ⁸⁾THEN WE LOOKED AT WHO IS ATTRACTED TO / CONFRONTED US WITH JESUS. ⁹⁾WE EXAMINED THE KINDS OF MIRACLES HE PERFORMED AND EXPLORED THEIR PURPOSE. ¹⁰⁾AND LAST WEEK WE LOOKED AT HIS DEATH / FINAL WEEK.

  - THIS WEEK WE LOOK AT THE RESURRECTION AND TRY TO EXAMINE IT AS IT MIGHT HAVE BEEN ON THAT DAY VS. HOW IT IS OBSERVED TODAY.

Session Eleven:
Resurrection: A Morning Beyond Belief

Questions To Consider

- How do we celebrate Easter today?

- What *really* happened on the first Easter?

- How do we deal with the doubts we may have about Jesus' resurrection?

WE MIGHT THINK OF THESE QUESTIONS TO FRAME OUR TALKS TODAY

79

WARM-UP

Warm-Up *(5–10 minutes)*

Easter!

> If possible, begin this exercise by playing a recording of Sandi Patty's "Was It a Morning Like This?"

As we begin to think about the first Easter morning, let's listen to a song by Sandi Patty that expresses some of the wonderment of what that morning must have been like.

> Play the song and solicit responses from the group to the following two questions.

❖ Does this song capture anything of what you think it may have been like?
❖ How did the song make you feel?

> Participant's Guide page 80

Let's go on to page 80 in your Participant's Guide. Think about some of the Easter experiences you have had in the past.

> Solicit responses from the group to the following questions.

❖ What Easter experiences have you had that have been truly meaningful?

> Possible Answers: A memory from childhood, a sunrise service, communion, a special musical presentation, a meaningful worship service

❖ What Easter experiences have you had that have been negative?

> Possible Answers: A memory from childhood; uncomfortable clothes; having to get up early for a sunrise service (maybe it was outside and really cold); baby ducks, chickens or rabbits that died; a boring musical presentation; a worship service that didn't capture the excitement of the occasion

Easter has become a very secular holiday in our culture for some. In this session we'll try to capture the significance of this important event in the life of Jesus.

Planning Notes

• TURN TO PAGE 80
 — TAKE 5-10 MINUTES TO JOT DOWN YOUR
 THOUGHTS RE THE TWO QUESTIONS... ALL
 OF US WILL SHARING AT LEAST ONE
 MEMORY -- GOOD OR BAD

 — ARE YOUR MEMORIES SECULAR?
 — IS THERE A WAY TO SEPARATE THE MATERIAL,
 THE COMMERCIAL, THE HOLIDAY FROM THE
 FAITH AND MIRACLE? TO EMPHASIZE THE
 LATTER OVER THE FORMER? IS THIS EVEN
 AN ISSUE IN YOUR HOME? SHOULD IT
 BE? (NO JUDGEMENT...JUST THOUGHT STARTERS)

[NEXT PAGE]

Session Eleven:
Resurrection: A Morning Beyond Belief

Questions To Consider

• How do we celebrate Easter today?

• What *really* happened on the first Easter?

• How do we deal with the doubts we may have about Jesus' resurrection?

79

---

80   The Jesus I Never Knew Participant's Guide

Easter!

What Easter experiences have you had that have been truly meaningful?

 — MY GODPARENTS BROUGHT ME A BELGIAN BUNNY
AND MY GODFATHER AND DAD BUILD A CAGE FOR IT THAT DAY
 — A SUNRISE SERVICE W/SUSIE ON AN AIRCRAFT CARRIER
(SUSIE HAD A BROKEN KNEE AND WE USED AN ORDNANCE ELEVATOR)

What Easter experiences have you had that have been negative?

 — A VERY SMALL TURNOUT AT A SUNRISE SERVICE
WITH AN UNINSPIRING SERVICE

 — MY LARGELY SECULAR VIEW OF EASTER
EVEN NOW

Content (30–35 minutes)

Bible Reading: Matthew 27:62–28:20 (2 minutes)

> You may choose to read this passage yourself, have someone else in the class read the entire portion, or break it up into smaller segments and have several different people read.

In order to have a frame of reference for our discussion in this session, let's read one of the accounts of Jesus' resurrection as it is found in Matthew 27:62–28:20.

Video Vignette (approximately 10 minutes)

> Participant's Guide page 81

In today's video segment Philip Yancey will share some thoughts on the impact of the Resurrection and then we'll have the opportunity to see two very different interpretations of it. As always there is space for you to take notes on page 81 of your Participant's Guide.

> View Video Vignette
> *Philip Yancey*—The impact of Jesus' resurrection
> *King of Kings*—Traditional portrayal of the resurrection scene
> *Cotton Patch Gospel*—Resurrection as experienced by one of the disciples

Class Response (8–10 minutes)

> Solicit responses from the group to the following questions.

1. Does your impression of the first Easter resemble in any way what was presented in the film clips?

2. What did you like or dislike about the movie interpretations?

3. What was your reaction to Philip Yancey's observation about who Jesus did and did *not* appear to? If Jesus were to live and die in the twentieth century, to whom do you think he would appear? Who would be left out?

– WHO WOULD JESUS APPEAR BEFORE?

    – BELIEVERS IN HIS LIFE

    – HE WOULD NOT TRY TO "WIN" OVER NON-BELIEVERS IN THE 9TH HOUR

– LEFT OUT?

    – THOSE WHO NEED TO HAVE FAITH

Planning Notes

- BIBLE READING
  - EACH PERSON READ TWO VERSES
    - MATTHEW 27:62 - 28:20
    - MARK 15:42 - 16:20
    - LUKE 23:50 - 24:53
    - JOHN 19:38 - 20:31

  - IN PREPARATION FOR THE VIDEOS
  - NOTE THAT THERE ARE SUBTLE DIFFERENCES
    - ADDITIONAL DETAILS
    - OMISSIONS
    - VARIATION IN THE TELLING
    - PROOF THERE IS NO SEAMLESS CONSPIRACY...

- VIDEOS
  - GO TO QUESTIONS ⊛

---

80   The Jesus I Never Knew Participant's Guide

Easter!

What Easter experiences have you had that have been truly meaningful?

What Easter experiences have you had that have been negative?

Session Eleven   81

Video Notes

Philip Yancey

King of Kings

Cotton Patch Gospel

Small Group Discussion (10–12 minutes)

Participant's Guide pages 82 and 83

Let's continue our discussion in groups of four. Turn to pages 82 and 83 in your Participant's Guide where you will find a set of questions.

We'll take about 10 minutes to work on this exercise.

Allow participants 10 minutes to work. Let them know when they have 1 minute remaining.

Summary (1 minute)

Participant's Guide page 84

Hopefully this session has triggered in you some thought about Easter and its significance in your life. The Bible clearly tells us that Jesus did rise from the dead, but what was it like to *be* there?! It's such an incredible occurrence that I'm sure we've all entertained some doubts along the way about the validity of such an event. But Christian faith rests on Jesus' resurrection as a fact, a fact we can count on and a promise of more good news to come.

I would encourage you to read chapter eleven in the book as Philip Yancey's insights may challenge and encourage you to think about this significant aspect of Jesus' life in a new way.

In our next session we'll take a closer look at Jesus' ascension.

6/15

PRAYER REQUESTS

- DAVE... PRAISE FOR A CAR BEING DELIVERED ('93 FORD EXPLORER)... RESPONSES TO REQUEST FOR HELP W/ HIS FINANCES
  ... CONTINUED UNSPOKEN REQUESTS AND DECISION-MAKING (VOCATION)

- SCOTT... PRAISE FOR LEADING A GRIEF SESSION @ A FOB

- MIKE... JEFF'S EMOTIONAL WELL-BEING/HAPPINESS

- SUSAN... ANNUAL CONFERENCE -- FAMILY HOLDS UP... BUSY FAMILY WK

Planning Notes

- SMALL GROUPS (2)

    - LOOK @ EACH QUESTION
        - GROUP 1 > QUESTION 1 ⎫ SHARE
        - GROUP 2 > QUESTION 2 ⎭ THOUGHTS

    - DO YOU BELIEVE IN THE RESURRECTION?
    - HOW MIGHT YOU HAVE REACTED?
    - IMAGINE SOMEONE YOU LOVE RETURNING FM DEATH? HOW MIGHT YOU REACT?

- SOLICIT PRAYER REQUESTS

- CLOSING PRAYER

---

82   The Jesus I Never Knew Participant's Guide

Small Group Discussion

1. The first Christians staked everything on the Resurrection, so much so that the apostle Paul told the Corinthians, "And if Christ has not been raised, our preaching is useless and so is your faith." Did it *really* happen—this event, apart from which our faith is useless? How can we be sure?

- YES. MY FAITH IS NOT USELESS (IT GUIDES MY LIFE, GIVES ME COMFORT, PROVIDES ANSWERS THE TANGIBLE WORLD CANNOT) THEREFORE CHRIST WAS RAISED.

- I AM SURE BECAUSE I CHOOSE TO BELIEVE. THINGS OF FAITH CANNOT BE PROVEN... IT IS THE NATURE OF FAITH... SO I CAN BE SURE WITHOUT THE "HOW"

2. In his book Philip Yancey writes, "One detail in the Easter stories has always intrigued me. Why did Jesus keep the scars from his crucifixion? Presumably he could have had any resurrected body he wanted, and yet he chose one identifiable mainly by scars that could be seen and touched. Why?" Do you have any ideas?

- YANCY: A REMINDER OF JESUS' UNNATURAL STATE ON EARTH... OF CONFINEMENT AND SUFFERING. A COMFORT THAT THOUGH SCARS ARE REAL/PERMANENT THEY WILL STOP HURTING AND WE WILL EVENTUALLY HEAL FROM OUR PAIN/SUFFERING

Session Eleven   83

3. Would you, like Thomas, have had to see Jesus to really believe he was risen—or would you have believed your friends and trusted that they were telling you the truth?

4. Think about your typical Easter celebration. What do you do on Easter? Does what you do reflect the importance of the Resurrection and the fact that this day defines your faith? Can you think of ways to make the celebration more significant?

---

84   The Jesus I Never Knew Participant's Guide

Summary

In this session we:

- Discussed some of the ways we presently celebrate Easter.

- Examined what *really* happened on that first Easter.

- Focused on some of the doubts we have about Jesus' resurrection.

> #### Suggested Reading
>
> For more thoughts on this session's topic, read
> "Resurrection: A Morning Beyond Belief,"
> chapter 11 of *The Jesus I Never Knew*.

Session Twelve:
Ascension:
A Blank Blue Sky

Before You Lead

Synopsis

If Easter Sunday was the most exciting day of the disciples' lives, for Jesus it was probably the day of Ascension. He, the Creator, who had descended so far and given up so much, was now heading home.

On the day Jesus ascended, the disciples stood around dumb-founded, like children who have lost their parents. They stood and gazed, not knowing how to go on or what to do next. Like the disciples' eyes, mine ache for a pure glimpse of the One who ascended. Why, I ask again, did he have to leave?

All along he had planned to depart to carry on his work in other bodies. Their bodies. Our bodies. The new body of Christ. The church, after all, is where God now lives. What Jesus brought to a few—healing, grace, the good-news message of God's love—the church can bring to all.

All through my own quest for Jesus has run a counterpoint theme: my need to strip away layers of dust and grim applied *by the church itself*. Many, far too many, abandon the quest for Christ entirely; repelled by the church, they never make it to Jesus.

Why don't we look more like the church Jesus described? Why do *I* so poorly resemble him? I offer three observations that help me come to terms with what has transpired since Jesus' ascension.

- The church has brought light as well as darkness. In the name of Jesus, people like Saint Francis, Mother Teresa, Wilberforce, General Booth, Dorothy Day, and others—educators, urban ministers, doctors and nurses, linguists, relief workers, ecologists—have served all over the world for little pay and less fame. God's hands on earth have reached wider since the Ascension.

- Jesus takes full responsibility for the constituent parts of his body. I take hope as I observe Jesus together with his disciples. Never did they disappoint him more than on the night of his betrayal. Yet it was then, says John, that Jesus "showed them the full extent of his love" (John 13:1), and then that he conferred on them a kingdom.

- The problem of the church is no different than the problem of one solitary Christian. How can an unholy assortment of men and women be the body of Christ? I answer with a different question: How can one sinful man, myself, be accepted as a child of God? One miracle makes possible the other.

Flannery O'Connor responded to a complaint about the church by saying,

> You are asking that man return at once to the state God created him in ... Christ was crucified on earth and the Church is crucified in time ... All human nature vigorously resists grace because grace changes us and the change is painful. Priests resist it as well as others. To have the Church be what you want it to be would require the continuous miraculous meddling of God in human affairs.

With a few exceptions, God, whose nature is self-living love, has chosen to allow himself to be "crucified in time" as his Son was on earth. Christ bears the wounds of the church, his body, just as he bore the wounds of crucifixion. I sometimes wonder which have hurt worse.

Session Outline

  I. Introduction
     Welcome
     Prayer
     Review

 II. Warm-Up
     The Ascension

III. Content
     Video Vignette
     Class Response
     Bible Study

 IV. Summary

Materials

No additional materials are needed for this session.

Recommended Reading

"Ascension: A Blank Blue Sky," chapter 12 of *The Jesus I Never Knew*

Session Twelve:
Ascension:
A Blank Blue Sky

Introduction *(3 Minutes)*

Welcome

> Call the group together.
> Welcome the participants to session 12 of *The Jesus I Never Knew* course:
> "Ascension: A Blank Blue Sky."

Prayer

Dear Jesus, once again we have gathered to take a look at your life and learn from it. As we study today the last event of your life on earth, help us to understand *why* you had to leave and how it makes a difference in each of us in how we carry out your work. We give this time to you. In your name we pray. Amen.

Review

In our last session we studied what for many is probably the most exciting day of Jesus' life—his resurrection. We had the opportunity to reflect on our own Easter experiences and then to compare those experiences with the actual account of Jesus' resurrection. We discussed some of the doubts we encounter in the Resurrection.

> Participant's Guide page 85

In this session we will be studying what Philip Yancey says may be one of the most exciting days in Jesus' life for Jesus himself. He, the Creator, who had descended so far and given up so much, was now heading home. How did Jesus' ascension affect his disciples, how has it affected the church, and how are we personally responding to the last words he spoke to his disciples, those of the Great Commission?

Planning Notes

• WELCOME
 - ONLY TWO MORE SESSIONS
 - LET'S FINISH STRONG AND
   TRY TO STRENGTHEN OUR
   NUMBERS
 - HOW WAS FATHER'S DAY?

•

- PRAYER

• REVIEW
 - WE MOVE TO THE TIME
   THAT JESUS LEAVES
   HIS EARTHLY WALK
 - IT HAS BEEN A CHRONOLOGICAL
   EXAMINATION AND WE GET
   CLOSER TO OUR EXPERIENCES
   OF TODAY

 - TODAY IS LITTLE SCRIPTURE
   AND LOTS OF QUESTIONS
   FOR US TO CONSIDER AND
   OPPORTUNITIES TO SHARE
   OUR THOUGHTS

Session Twelve:
Ascension:
A Blank Blue Sky

Questions To Consider

A RETURN TO GOD'S KINGDOM TO SIT AT THE RIGHT HAND OF GOD, HIS FATHER

• What was the ascension of Jesus and what impact has it had on the church?

CREATED THE "NEW" BODY OF CHRIST ON THE CHURCH AND ON US

• How are we fulfilling the "Great Commission?"

① WHAT JESUS BROUGHT TO THE FEW — HEALING, GRACE, THE GOOD-NEWS MSG OF GOD'S LOVE — THE CHURCH (WHICH IS THE NEW BODY OF CHRIST AND IS ALSO EACH OF US) CAN NOW BRING TO ALL.

② "I TELL YOU THE TRUTH, WHATEVER YOU DID FOR ONE OF THE LEAST OF THESE BROTHERS OF MINE, YOU DID FOR ME" (PG 231)

③ "KILLING JESUS WAS LIKE TRYING TO DESTROY A DANDELION SEED HEAD BY BLOWING ON IT" (PG 226)

Warm-Up *(5 minutes)*

The Ascension

| Participant's Guide page 86 |

Turn to page 86 in your Participant's Guide. As we begin our study of Jesus' ascension, let's consider these three questions.

| Solicit responses from the group to the following questions. |

◆ What was the ascension of Jesus?

(There may be those in your group who do not know the answer to this question!)

◆ Think of a time you had to say good-by to someone you really cared about. How did you feel? What did you do? How do you think the disciples felt as they watched Jesus return to heaven?

◆ How do you think you might have responded to this amazing event if you had been there?

Content *(35 minutes)*

Video Vignette *(approximately 10 minutes)*

| Participant's Guide page 87 |

As we consider Jesus' ascension, the video segments presented in today's session will give us a great deal to think about.

> View Video Vignette
> *Philip Yancey*—How can it be good that Jesus leaves us here alone? We are the only way now for the world to get to know God.
> *Gospel Road*—Jesus' death around the world
> *Jesus*—Jesus' appearances to the disciples, the Great Commission, the Ascension

Class Response *(10 minutes)*

| Solicit responses from the group to the following questions. |

1. What is your reaction to the scenes portrayed in *The Gospel Road?* What message is the filmmaker trying to convey?

2. What did you think of the scenes in the *Jesus* clip? How have you envisioned the Ascension in the past? If you were making a movie, what would you show?

3. What is your response to Philip Yancey's assertion that it's now up to *us?*

Planning Notes

* TURN TO PAGE 86
  - TALK AS A GROUP AND SHARE
    ANSWERS W/ ALL

* WATCH VIDEOS
  - POSE QUESTIONS (#) ON EACH

    1:15:44

The Ascension

What was the ascension of Jesus?

A RETURN TO THE KINGDOM OF HEAVEN
TO SIT @ THE RH OF GOD, HIS FATHER

Think of a time you had to say good-bye to someone you really cared about. How did you feel? What did you do? How do you think the disciples felt as they watched Jesus return to heaven?

- SAD, ALONE, LOST
- CRIED... "GOT BACK ON THE HORSE"
- ALONE, LOST, FRIGHTENED, UNSURE WHAT TO DO NEXT

How do you think you might have responded to this amazing event if you had been there?

- PLOTTED MY NEXT MOVE

Video Notes
Philip Yancey

Gospel Road

Jesus

Bible Study *(15 minutes)*

> Participant's Guide pages 88 and 89

We're going to continue our discussion of the Ascension in a more personal way in smaller groups. Let's break into groups of four and turn to pages 88 and 89 in the Participant's Guide. Begin by reading together the assigned passage in Matthew and then work your way through the questions.

> Give the groups 15 minutes to discuss. Let them know when they have 1 minute remaining.

If you made it to the end of the questions, you've discovered that once again we've moved from a basic knowledge discussion to a personal confrontation with who Jesus is and what difference that makes in our lives.

Summary *(1 minute)*

> Participant's Guide page 90

In this session we've discussed an event in Jesus' life that many of us often overlook, but one that has a significant impact on us as Christians. Jesus left this earth and we are here to carry on his work. What difference does that make in *your* life?

In our next session we'll take a closer look at our lives without Christ here to personally guide us. Our topic will be his kingdom.

6/22

Conc. Bill Johnson — recover / handle well
       Becky Hott — successful pregnancy

Barn: Routine
      Unspoken prayer
      Communion — what is God's message / direction for me — vocation for
         Tim in teaching credentials — praise to Scott for making the
         commitment from around the world.

Planning Notes

- SCRIPTURE
  - MATTHEW 28: 18-20

- SOLICIT PRAYER REQUESTS

- CLOSING PRAYER

A

Call Dave ... Wednesday

Bible Study

Read Matthew 28:18–20

1. In his book Philip Yancey writes: "I have concluded that the Ascension represents my greatest struggle of faith—not whether it happened, but why. Would it not have been better if the Ascension had never happened? If Jesus had stayed on earth, he could answer our questions, solve our doubts, mediate our disputes of doctrine and policy. However, Jesus played his part and then left. Now it is up to us." What do you think?

IF JESUS HAD STAYED, "FAITH" WOULD NOT BE POSSIBLE .. THE "PROOF" WOULD BE THERE AND IT WOULD BE MORE COMPLIANCE WITH THE OBVIOUS. GOD INTENDED FOR US TO CHOOSE TO BELIEVE IN THE ABSENCE OF PROOF

2. What is the Great Commission? What does it mean to fulfill the Great Commission? As a church? As an individual? Do you think the Great Commission is realistic in our world?

SEE PG 143 NOTES

---

3. When are you most likely to compare God's call to you with his call to someone else? Do you ever shy away from service to God because you're intimidated by someone else or simply don't see a place for yourself? What do you need to do to begin to take Jesus' message seriously in your own life?

① WHEN THERE IS IMBALANCE IN REWARD, OR TOO HIGH A PRICE TO PAY, OR TOO GREAT OF A SACRIFICE DEMANDED

② YES ... CHALLENGED TO BE AN EVANGELIST... FEAR OF BRANDING / OFFENSE AS A "BIBLE THUMPER"

③ I DO. BUT I CAN DO MORE. I NEED TO BE LESS WORRIED ABOUT REJECTION AND SPREAD THE WORD

Summary

In this session we:

- Ascertained what the ascension of Jesus was and what kind of impact it had on the disciples and our world.

- Examined our lives in light of the Great Commission.

Suggested Reading

For more thoughts on this session's topic, read "Ascension: A Blank Blue Sky," chapter 12 of *The Jesus I Never Knew.*

Session Thirteen:
Kingdom: Wheat Among the Weeds

Before You Lead

Synopsis

Each fall the church I attended during my childhood sponsored a prophecy conference. Silver-haired men of national repute would sketch the movements of million-strong armies that would soon converge on Israel. Nuclear war would break out, and the planet would teeter on the brink of annihilation until at the last second Jesus himself would return to lead the armies of righteousness.

What sticks with me is not so much the particulars of prophecy as their emotional effect on me. I grew up at once terrified and desperately hopeful. Later, as I read church history, I learned that often before—during the first decades of Christianity, the end of the tenth century, the late 1300's, the Napoleanic era, during World War I, the time of the Axis of Hitler and Mussolini—visions of the end times had bubbled to the surface. Each time, Christians went through a passionate cycle of fear, hope, and then sheepish disillusionment. The end times had not arrived after all.

In Jesus' day, Jews were poring over the same passages from Daniel and Ezekiel that would later figure so prominently in the prophecy conferences of my childhood. We disagreed on some details, yet our visions of the Messiah matched: we expected a conquering hero. "The kingdom of heaven is near," Jesus proclaimed in his very first message (Matt. 4:17), awakening the image of a political leader who would arise, take charge, and defeat the most powerful empire ever known. But to the crowd's dismay, it became clear that Jesus was talking about a strangely different kind of kingdom. Jesus announced a kingdom that meant denying yourself, taking up your cross, renouncing wealth, even loving your enemies. As he elaborated, the crowd's expectations crumbled.

Jesus never offered a clear definition of the kingdom; instead, he imparted his vision of it indirectly, through a series of stories. His choice of images is telling: everyday sketches of farming, fishing, women baking bread, merchants buying pearls. As I review the parables of the kingdom, I realize how far my own understanding has drifted from such homespun images. I tend to envision the same kind of kingdom the Jews did: a visible, powerful kingdom. I think of Constantine leading his troops, crosses emblazoned on their armor, with the slogan "By this sign conquer." I think of the armies at the prophecy conferences. Obviously I need to listen again to Jesus' description of the kingdom of God.

Those of us in the twentieth century, an era that has few literal kings, conceive of kingdoms in terms of power and polarization. We are the children of revolution. But Jesus' message of the kingdom had little in common with the politics of polarization. He invoked a different kind of power: love, not coercion.

Sheep among wolves, a tiny seed in the garden, yeast in bread dough, salt in meat—Jesus' own metaphors of the kingdom describe a kind of "secret force" that works from within. He said nothing of a triumphant church sharing power with the authorities. The kingdom of God appears to work best as a minority movement in opposition to the kingdom of this world. When it grows beyond that, the kingdom subtly changes in nature. In fact, problems seem to arise when the church becomes too external and gets cozy with government. As one U.S. legislative aide said after observing China's underground church, "They fervently pray for their leaders but maintain a careful independence ... I have seen more than a few [American] believers trade their Christian birthright for a mess of earthly pottage. We must continually ask ourselves: Is our first aim to change our government or to see lives in and out of government changed for Christ?"

In some important ways, the kingdom has not fully come. It is "now" and also "not yet," present and also future. Only at Christ's second coming will the kingdom of God appear in all its fullness. In the meantime we work toward a better future, always glancing back to the Gospels for a template of what that future will be like. We in the church, Jesus' successors, are left with the task of displaying the signs of the kingdom of God, and the watching world will judge the merits of the kingdom by us. We live in a transition time, marked here and there, now and then, with clues of what God will someday achieve in perfection. The reign of God is breaking in the world, and we can be its heralds.

Session Outline

    I. Introduction
      Welcome
      Prayer
      Review

    II. Warm-Up
      Jesus' Second Coming

    III. Content
      Video Vignette
      Class Response
      Bible Study

    IV. Summary

Materials

No additional materials are needed for this session.

Recommended Reading

"Kingdom: Wheat Among the Weeds," chapter 13 of *The Jesus I Never Knew*

Session Thirteen:
Kingdom: Wheat Among the Weeds

Introduction *(3 minutes)*

Welcome

> Call the group together.
> Welcome the participants to session 13 of *The Jesus I Never Knew* course: "Kingdom: Wheat Among the Weeds."

Prayer

Jesus, we come before you as your humble servants. We've learned so much about who you are and how it can make a difference in who we are. Give us insight into your Word today as we consider your kingdom. May we be the kind of people who are truly wheat among the weeds. Amen.

Review

In the last session we studied Jesus' last event while he was on earth—his ascension. We thought about what kind of impact it had on our world and considered how we might carry out his last commandment to the disciples—the Great Commission.

> Participant's Guide page 91

In this session we're going to be looking at our lives in light of Jesus' physical absence from us. What *is* the *kingdom* and how can we best live it out in our world?

150

Planning Notes

○ WELCOME
— DAVE -- SORRY WE DIDN'T
    HOOK UP -- LEFT MSGS
— ONE MORE CLASS LEFT
    — WE WON'T MEET NEXT WK
    — NEED TO DISCUSS WHAT'S
    NEXT FOR US...
— HAVE A GREAT 4TH OF JULY

○ PRAYER

○ REVIEW
— WE'VE TRACKED FROM OUR
    PERCEPTIONS TO HIS BIRTH
    THROUGH HIS DEATH
— HIS RESURRECTION TO HIS
    ASCENSION
— NOW FOR THE FIRST TIME
    WE TALK ABOUT OUR
    TIME WITH JESUS'
    PHYSICAL ABSENCE

○ AS WE GO THROUGH OUR
    VIDEOS AND OUR DISCUSSION,
    KEEP THESE TWO QUESTIONS
    IN MIND

Session Thirteen:
Kingdom: Wheat Among the Weeds

Questions To Consider

- What *is* the kingdom?

- How can we best live out the kingdom and express Jesus' love?

91

Warm-Up *(5 minutes)*

Jesus' Second Coming

> Participant's Guide page 92

Let's turn to page 92 in the Participant's Guide. Jesus promised another kingdom. Let's discuss together the two questions found here as we begin our discussion of the kingdom.

> Solicit responses from the group to the following questions.

❖ What comes to your mind when you think about the "end times"?
❖ What meaning does Jesus' second coming have for you? Does it affect your life at all?

Content *(35 minutes)*

Video Vignette *(approximately 10 minutes)*

> Participant's Guide page 93

Our video segment today is a little unusual. Philip Yancey will present some information about the kingdom as he understands it, and then we will see two very different scenes depicting what it means to live out the kingdom.

> View Video Vignette
> *Philip Yancey*—Jesus' revolution is not political. The church can thrive anywhere.
> *The Gospel According to St. Matthew*—Jesus' instructions to the disciples
> *Son of Man*—"Turn the other cheek"

Class Response *(10 minutes)*

> Solicit responses from the group to the following questions.

1. Do you agree or disagree with Philip Yancey's assertion that Jesus' revolution is not primarily political? Did the film clips portray a political or nonpolitical message?

2. Do you think *The Gospel According to St. Matthew* portrayal is realistic? What do you like or dislike about the way Jesus is portrayed here?

3. In the *Son of Man* scene, we see a young girl refusing to respond to the cruelty of Pilate. Have you ever been in a situation that warranted that kind of "turning the other cheek?" How do we usually respond to these types of situations?

Planning Notes

○ TURN TO PAGE 92
— TALK ABOUT EACH QUESTION AS A
GROUP

• VIDEOS
— SEE QUESTIONS AND NOTES
— FOCUS ON #1, #4 AND (#3)

Jesus' Second Coming

What comes to your mind when you think about the "end times"?

— JUDGEMENT DAY
— EQUATES TO JESUS' SECOND COMING

What meaning does Jesus' second coming have for you? Does it affect your life at all?

① — I WILL BE JUDGED ON HOW I LIVED
MY LIFE. WAS I A GOOD PERSON...
A PERSON OF FAITH...A BELIEVER

② YES. I LIVE AS IF I'M BEING JUDGED

Video Notes
Philip Yancey

The Gospel According to St. Matthew

Son of Man

(handwritten margin note, top left) IS IT HARD? I DON'T THINK SO. — IT IS HARD TO LIVE AND PREACH BECAUSE THE WORLD IS NOT ACCEPTING MEANS

4. Why is the message of Christ's kingdom so hard for us to put into practice?

Bible Study *(15 minutes)*

> Participant's Guide pages 94 and 95

For the last several sessions we've used our remaining time to discuss our topic on a more personal level. We're going to do the same thing again. Let's get into groups of four and work through the Bible study provided for us on pages 94 and 95 of the Participant's Guide.

> Give the groups 15 minutes to share. Let them know when they have 1 minute remaining.

Communicating the love of Jesus has proven to be a difficult assignment throughout this course. As you go through the next week, try to keep in mind some of the things we've discussed today.

Summary *(1 minute)*

> Participant's Guide page 96

In this session we attempted to define the kingdom of Jesus. We also began to think about how we can best live out the kingdom in our world and express Jesus' love as we deal with difficult people and situations. Answers for these topics are very elusive and, as we're finding week after week, they require on-going reflection on our part.

In the next session we'll conclude this course as we wrap up and reflect upon the difference Jesus makes.

(handwritten notes at bottom of page)

6/25

→ For Susan — challenging time and work ... come back w/ vision

Dave: Unspoken prayer ... faith of the group ... need real sleep (CPAP machine is broken) — for the routine of studying .. Tim Kass

Sure: Bill Johnson (tumor)

(a disease P&P in a wheelchair — emotion)

Lynne: Safety during trip to Hawaii/Maui (and good health)

Scott: Sister — 7 months pregnant .. Christine

Planning Notes

○ BIBLE STUDIES (PG 94)

   — ASK FOR VOLUNTEER READERS

   — DISCUSS ANSWERS

   • (PG 95)

   — ASK FOR A LEADER

   — DISCUSS ANSWERS

• SOLICIT PRAYER REQUESTS

○ DISCUSS NEXT SMALL GROUP

○ REMINDER: NEXT MTG IS 13 JUL

○ CLOSING PRAYER

Bible Study

Read   Matthew 13:24–30, 36–43
        John 18:36–37
        Matthew 24:4–14

1. What is Jesus teaching us about his *kingdom* in these passages?

ANS

— KINGDOM IS INSIDE EACH OF US ... TO BE PRODUCTIVE, POSITIVE, KIND, CARING, GIVING (THE WHEAT)

— IT IS THE GOSPEL OF SALVATION FOR THOSE JUDGED WELL

— IT IS ABOUT JUDGEMENT ... SALVATION VS DAMNATION

2. Why is this message so hard for us to grasp? As you think carefully about the passages you just read, in what ways does this message go against what we often *hear* about the kingdom of God? In what ways have you heard this message distorted?

Read John 17:20–23

1. How do you communicate Jesus' message of love?

— BY BEING A GOOD EXAMPLE TO OTHERS

— TEACHING MY CHILDREN ABOUT PRINCIPLES

— OBEY 10 COMMANDMENTS / GOLDEN RULES

— BEING (TRYING TO BE) A DISCIPLE FOR GOD

2. What are some of the "evils of our society?" How can we confront these things and still communicate the love of Christ?

— MURDER, LIARS,

    ↳ DILEMMA: CAPITAL PUNISHMENT

— FALSE PROPHETS ~ JONES, KORESH, JEFFERIES
               JIM DAVID WARRON

Summary

In this session we:

• Discussed the kingdom from the perspective of what we have learned from Philip Yancey and from our own understanding of the Scripture.

• Reflected upon how we can best live out the kingdom and express Jesus' love.

> ### Suggested Reading
>
> For more thoughts on this session's topic, read
> "Kingdom: Wheat Among the Weeds,"
> chapter 13 of *The Jesus I Never Knew*.

Session Fourteen:
The Difference He Makes

Before You Lead

Synopsis

I conclude my survey of Jesus with as many questions as answers. I now have a built-in suspicion against all attempts to categorize Jesus, to box him in. Jesus is radically unlike anyone else who has ever lived. The difference, in Charles Williams' phrase, is the difference between "one who is an example of living and one who is the life itself."

To sum up what I have learned about Jesus, I offer a series of impressions. They do not form a whole picture by any means, but these are the acts of Jesus' life that challenge me and, I suspect, will never cease to challenge me.

A sinless friend of sinners. When Jesus came to earth, demons recognized him, the sick flocked to him, and sinners doused his feet and head with perfume. Meanwhile he offended pious Jews with their strict preconceptions of what God should be like. Their rejection makes me wonder: Could religious types be doing just the reverse now? Could we be perpetuating an image of Jesus that fits our pious expectations but does not match the person portrayed so vividly in the Gospels?

Jesus was a friend of sinners. Yet Jesus himself was not a sinner. I view with amazement Jesus' uncompromising blend of graciousness toward sinners and hostility toward sin, because in much of church history I see virtually the opposite. For example, nowadays many of the same Christians who hotly condemn homosexuality, which Jesus did not mention, disregard his straightforward commands against divorce. All too often sinners feel unloved by a church that, in turn, keeps altering its definition of sin—exactly the opposite of Jesus' pattern. Something has gone awry.

The God-Man. Jesus' audacious claims about himself—"I and the Father are one" (John 10:30)—pose what may be the central problem of all history, the dividing point between Christianity and other religions. Although Muslims—and increasingly, Jews—respect Jesus as a great teacher and prophet, no Muslim can imagine Mohammed claiming to be Allah, any more than a Jew can imagine Moses claiming to be Yahweh. Hindus believe in many incarnations but not one Incarnation, while Buddhists have no categories in which to conceive of a sovereign God becoming a human being.

Could Jesus' disciples have backfilled his teaching to include such brazen claims, as part of their conspiracy to launch a new religion? Unlikely. The disciples were inept conspirators, and in fact the Gospels portray them as resistant to the very idea of Jesus' divinity. Yet by the time the Gospels were written, the disciples regarded Jesus as the Word who was God, through whom all things were made. As I have studied the Gospels, I have come to agree with C. S. Lewis, who wrote, in a famous passage in *Mere Christianity,*

> A man who was merely a man and said the sort of things Jesus said would not be a great moral teacher. He would either be a lunatic—on the level with the man who says he is a poached egg—or else he would be the Devil of Hell. You must make your choice. Either this man was, and is, the Son of God; or else a madman or something worse. (*Mere Christianity,* 56)

Portrait of God. George Buttrick, former chaplain at Harvard, recalls that students would come into his office and declare, "I don't believe in God." Buttrick would give this disarming reply: "Sit down and tell me what kind of God you don't believe in. I probably don't believe in that God either." And then he would talk about Jesus, the corrective to all our assumptions about God.

Martin Luther encouraged his students to flee the hidden God and run to Christ, and now I know why. If I use a magnifying glass to examine a fine painting, the object in the center of the glass stays crisp and clear, while around the edges the view grows increasingly distorted. For me, Jesus has become the focal point. When I speculate about such imponderables as the problem of pain or providence versus free will, everything becomes fuzzy. But if I look at Jesus himself, at how he treated actual people in pain, at his calls to free and diligent action, clarity is restored. I can worry myself into a state of spiritual ennui over questions like, "What good does it do to pray if God already knows everything?" Jesus silences such questions: he prayed; so should we.

The Lover. Jesus reveals a God who comes in search of us, a God who makes room for our freedom even when it costs the Son's life, a God who is vulnerable. Above all, Jesus reveals a God who is love. Love has never been a normal way of describing what happens between human beings and their God. Not once does the Qur'an apply the word *love* to God. Aristotle stated bluntly, "It would be eccentric for anyone to claim that he loved Zeus." In dazzling contrast, the Christian Bible affirms, "God is love" (I John 4:16) and cites love as the main reason Jesus came to earth: "This is how God showed his love among us: He sent his one and only Son into the world that we might live through him" (I John 4:9).

I remember a long night in O'Hare Airport, waiting impatiently for a flight that was delayed for five hours. I happened to be next to a wise woman who was traveling to the same conference. I was writing the book *Disappointment with God* at the time, and I felt burdened by other people's pains and sorrows, doubts and unanswered prayers. My companion listened to me in silence for a very long time, and then out of nowhere she asked a question that has always stayed with me. "Philip, do you ever just let God love you?" she said. "It's pretty important, I think." I realized with a start that she had brought to light a gaping hole in my spiritual life. For all my absorption in the Christian faith, I had missed the most important message of all. The story of Jesus is a story of celebration, a story of love. Jesus embodies the promise of a God who will go to any length to win us back. Not the least of Jesus' accomplishments is that he made us somehow lovable to God.

Portrait of Humanity. When a light is brought into a room, what was a window becomes also a mirror reflecting back the contents of that room. In Jesus not only do we have a window to God, we also have a mirror of ourselves. Human beings were, after all, created in the image of God; Jesus reveals what that image should look like.

God's character did not permit the option of simply declaring about this defective planet, "It doesn't matter." God's Son had to encounter evil personally in a way that perfect deity had never before encountered evil. He had to forgive by taking on our sin. He had to defeat death by dying. He had to learn sympathy for human beings by becoming one. Because of the Incarnation, Hebrews implies, God hears our prayers in a new way, having lived here and having prayed as a weak and vulnerable human being.

The Wounded Healer. The author and preacher Tony Campolo delivers a stirring sermon adapted from an elderly black pastor at his church in Philadelphia. "It's Friday, but Sunday's Comin'" is the title of the sermon, and once you know the title, you know the whole sermon. The disciples who lived through both days, Friday and Sunday, never doubted God again. They had learned that when God seems most absent, he may be closest of all; when God looks most powerless, he may be most powerful; when God looks most dead, he may be coming back to life.

Campolo skipped one day in his sermon, though. The other two days have earned names on the church calendar: Good Friday and Easter Sunday. Yet in a real sense, we live on Saturday, the day with no name. What the disciples experienced on a small scale—three days in grief over one man who had died on a cross—we now live through on a cosmic scale. Human history grinds on between the time of promise and fulfillment. Easter opened up a crack in a decaying universe, sealing the promise that someday God will enlarge the miracle of Easter to a cosmic scale.

Session Outline

    I. Introduction
       Welcome
       Prayer
       Review

    II. Warm-Up (Not included for this session)

    III. Content
       Six Facets of Jesus' Life
       Small Group Discussion
       Video Vignette
       Class Response/Course Closure

    IV. Summary

Materials

No additional materials are needed for this session.

Recommended Reading

"The Difference He Makes," chapter 14 of *The Jesus I Never Knew*

Session Fourteen:
The Difference He Makes

Introduction *(3 Minutes)*

Welcome

> Call the group together.
> Welcome the participants to the final session of *The Jesus I Never Knew* course: "The Difference He Makes."

Prayer

Dear Jesus, thank you for coming to earth, for living a life that was a message of love and grace, for dying a sinner's death for each one of us, for conquering death through your resurrection, and for leaving us with the hope of your presence and power as we await your second coming. As we consider your life as a whole and try to reflect on what we've learned throughout this course, help us to take something with us that is significant and will have a lasting impact on those around us. In your name we pray. Amen.

Review

In our previous time together, we discussed Christ's kingdom and tried to identify some of the ways we can communicate his kingdom to those around us.

> Participant's Guide page 97

In the last session we are going to try to reflect on some of the themes that have run throughout this course. We'll also spend a little bit of time sharing some of the ways our thinking has been challenged and our lives have changed as we have experienced Jesus.

160

Planning Notes

• WELCOME
 — HOPE EVERYONE HAD A
   NICE 4TH OF JULY
 — GOOD TO HAVE SUSAN
   WITH US
 — AND AUDREY

 — LAST CLASS. WE'LL
   LEAVE SOME TIME
   FOR SUSAN TO TALK
   ABOUT OPTIONS TO
   CONTINUE MEETING

• PRAYER

• REVIEW
 — THIS WEEK WE HAVE
   AN OPPORTUNITY TO
   SHARE OUR THOUGHTS
   ON OUR UNDERSTANDING
   AND CHARACTERIZATION
   OF JESUS

 — TIME PERMITTING, WE
   CAN TALK ABOUT THE
   DIFFERENCE THIS COURSE
   HAS MADE ON YOUR
   UNDERSTANDING OF
   JESUS

 — NO SCRIPTURE TODAY

 — AS A STARTING POINT... TURN THE PAGE

Session Fourteen:
The Difference He Makes

Questions To Consider

• How does Philip Yancey characterize Jesus?

• What difference has this course made on my understanding of Jesus?

97

Warm-Up (not included in this session)

To allow more time for interaction with one another as we seek to bring closure to our time together, we'll jump right into the topic material.

Content (approximately 40 minutes)

Six Facets of Jesus' Life

Participant's Guide page 98

The explanation paragraphs are taken from the synopsis section found at the beginning of this session.

Turn to page 98 in your Participant's Guide. As Philip Yancey concluded this study with his class in Chicago, he came up with six characterizations or facets of Jesus' life. They do not form a whole picture of who Jesus is, but they are aspects of Jesus' character that challenge us.

❖ Jesus is:

❖ 1. The sinless FRIEND of SINNERS.

Jesus was a friend of sinners. Yet Jesus himself was not a sinner. He had an amazing ability to communicate an uncompromising blend of graciousness toward sinners *and* hostility toward sin. If we were to study church history, we would discover many examples of just the opposite. In our own culture today, for example, many of the same Christians who hotly condemn homosexuality, which Jesus did not mention, disregard his straightforward commands against divorce. All too often sinners feel unloved by a church that, in turn, keeps altering its definition of sin—exactly the opposite of Jesus' pattern.

❖ 2. The GOD-MAN.

Jesus' audacious claims about himself—"I and the Father are one" (John 10:30)—pose what may be the central problem of all history, the dividing point between Christianity and other religions. Although Muslims—and increasingly, Jews—respect Jesus as a great teacher and prophet, no Muslim can imagine Mohammed claiming to be Allah, any more than a Jew can imagine Moses claiming to be Yahweh. Hindus believe in many incarnations but not one Incarnation, while Buddhists have no categories in which to conceive of a sovereign God becoming a human being.

❖ 3. A portrait of GOD.

George Buttrick, former chaplain at Harvard, recalls that students would come into his office and declare, "I don't believe in God." Buttrick would give this disarming reply: "Sit down and tell me what kind of God you don't

Planning Notes

· TURN TO PAGE 98

— LET'S TRY TO FILL IN
THE BLANKS ON THIS PAGE
— THE SIX FACETS ARE
PH YANCY'S IMPRESSIONS.. THEY
ARE HIS DESCRIPTION OF THE
"ACTS OF JESUS' LIFE" THAT
CHALLENGE HIM. THEY ARE
NOT "A WHOLE PICTURE" OF
JESUS FOR YANCY, BUT SUM
UP WHAT HE HAS LEARNED.

— WE CAN TALK IN MORE
DETAIL ON EACH.

① A FRIEND OF SINNERS, BUT
NOT A SINNER, HIMSELF (THOUGH
HE DID BEND A FEW CONVENTIONS
OF HIS TIME — WORK ON THE
SABBATH, CLAIM TO BE THE
MESSIAH, ETC.)
— GRACIOUSNESS TOWARD
SINNERS, AND HOSTILITY
TOWARD SIN
— ARE SINNERS WELCOME IN
OUR CHURCH OR DO THEY
FEEL UNWELCOME OR SOMEHOW
LESS THAN OTHERS?
— IS RELIGION USED TO ADVOCATE
A MORAL VIEW, BUT UNBALANCED
(HOMOSEXUALITY V DIVORCE/ADULTERY)

98
The Jesus I Never Knew Participant's Guide

Six Facets of Jesus' Life

Jesus is:

1. The sinless FRIEND of SINNERS.

2. The GOD - MAN.

3. A portrait of GOD.

4. The _____.

5. A portrait of _____.

6. The _____ _____.

② THIS IS EMBODIED IN
JESUS' CLAIM TO BE THE MESSIAH
AND GOD.. "I AND THE FATHER
ARE ONE ".. NO OTHER RELIGION
HAS A FIGURE SUCH AS JESUS WITH
THIS TENET
— WHY IS THIS IMPORTANT TO US?
— GOD REVEALS HIMSELF TO US
— GOD RELATES TO US
— GOD LOVES US

NEXT PAGE

believe in. I probably don't believe in that God either." And then he would talk about Jesus, the corrective to all our assumptions about God.

◆ 4. The LOVER.

Jesus reveals a God who comes in search of us, a God who makes room for our freedom even when it costs the Son's life, a God who is vulnerable. Above all, Jesus reveals a God who is love.

The story of Jesus is a story of celebration, a story of love. Jesus embodies the promise of a God who will go to any length to win us back. Not the least of Jesus' accomplishments is that he made us somehow lovable to God.

◆ 5. A portrait of HUMANITY.

God's character did not permit the option of simply declaring about this defective planet, "It doesn't matter." God's Son had to encounter evil personally in a way that perfect deity had never before encountered evil. He had to forgive by taking on our sin. He had to defeat death by dying. He had to learn sympathy for human beings by becoming one. Because of the Incarnation, God hears our prayers in a new way, having lived here and having prayed as a weak and vulnerable human being.

◆ 6. The WOUNDED HEALER.

The author and preacher Tony Campolo delivers a stirring sermon adapted from an elderly black pastor at his church in Philadelphia. "It's Friday, but Sunday's Comin'" is the title of the sermon, and once you know the title, you know the whole sermon. The disciples who lived through both days, Friday and Sunday, never doubted God again. They had learned that when God seems most absent, he may be closest of all; when God looks most powerless, he may be most powerful; when God looks most dead, he may be coming back to life.

Campolo skipped one day in his sermon, though. The other two days have earned names on the church calendar: Good Friday and Easter Sunday. Yet in a real sense, we live on Saturday, the day with no name. What the disciples experienced on a small scale—three days in grief over one man who had died on a cross—we now live through on a cosmic scale. Human history grinds on between the time of promise and fulfillment. Easter opened up a crack in a decaying universe, sealing the promise that someday God will enlarge the miracle of Easter to a cosmic scale.

Small Group Discussion *(15 minutes)*

> Participant's Guide page 99

We're going to discuss this material in groups of four. Turn to page 99 in your Participant's Guide and work through the questions.

> Allow participants 15 minutes to discuss. Let them know when they have 1 minute remaining.

Planning Notes

③ - YANCY SAYS "[JESUS] IS WHO I WANT GOD TO BE"
- APOSTLE PAUL: "THE IMAGE OF THE INVISIBLE GOD"
- MARTIN LUTHER ENCOURAGED STUDENTS TO
  FLEE "THE HIDDEN GOD AND RUN TO CHRIST"... THIS
  IS THE FOCAL POINT TO FAITH
- ONLY THROUGH JESUS DO WE HAVE IMMEDIATE
  ACCESS TO GOD'S PRESENCE

④ - A GOD WHO LOVES AND YEARNS TO BE LOVED
- A GOD WHO COMES IN SEARCH OF US
- A GOD WHO MAKES ROOM FOR OUR FREEDOM
  EVEN WHEN IT COSTS THE SON'S LIFE
- A GOD WHO IS VULNERABLE
A GOD WHO LOVES AND IS FORGIVING IS NOT THE NORM...
TYPICALLY TRADITIONAL GODS JUDGE, REWARD OR PUNISH
AND ARE NOT ACCESSIBLE

⑤ ~ TO BE HUMAN
- SEE PG 270 .. FROM TWO EPISTLES
- PG 270 ... "UNDER ..." TO PG 271 ... "ALL THAT"
- JESUS LIVED AMONG US - NOW HE UNDERSTOOD .

⑥ THE CROSS GIVES HOPE WHEN THERE IS
   NO HOPE
   - SEE PAG 273
   - "THE MOST VILLAINOUS CRIME BECOMES
     OUR HEALING STRENGTH"
   - SEE PAGE 274 ... THOUGHTS?

---

98   The Jesus I Never Knew Participant's Guide

Six Facets of Jesus' Life

Jesus is:
1. The sinless FRIEND of SINNERS

2. The GOD - MAN .

3. A portrait of GOD .

4. The LOVER .

5. A portrait of HUMANITY .

6. The WOUNDED HEALER .

Session Fourteen   99

Small Group Discussion

1. Refer to the six facets of Jesus' life listed on the previous page.
   Which do you most identify with?

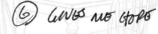

⑥ GIVES ME HOPE

2. One of the themes throughout this course has been Jesus' love. How
   does this square with your past understanding of Jesus? Have your
   views changed at all? Explain.

   JESUS LOVED THE SINNERS, RESONATED WITH
   THE SINNERS... THIS IS DIFFERENT THAN
   I IMAGINED -- THOUGHT HE LOVED THOSE
   WHO WERE FAITHFUL.

3. In his book Philip Yancey has written, "Jesus is radically unlike anyone else who has ever lived." Do you agree or disagree? Why did
   Jesus—his life and his message—have such a dramatic impact on
   his world? Why does it have an impact on our world?

① AGREE... NOT A CONQUEROR, NOT SELF-IMPORTANT (SORT
   OF)
   A SELF-PROCLAIMED MESSIAH, A MIRACLE
   WORKER FOR ALL TO SEE

② SO DIFFERENT... RADICAL

③ OUR FAITH IS DEFINED BY HIM

Let's get back into our large group and watch the last video segment.

Video Vignette *(approximately 2 minutes)*

> Participant's Guide page 100

In this session we will not see any film clips. We do have, however, a short summary from Philip Yancey.

> View Video Vignette
>
> *Philip Yancey*—The difference Jesus has made in Philip's life. However, what is more important is what difference he has made in *your* life.

Class Response/Course Closure *(12–15 minutes)*

> Participant's Guide page 101. Solicit responses from the group to the lead-in sentence.

Take a look at the lead-in sentence on page 101 of your Participant's Guide.

1. Would anyone be willing to share how they would conclude that phrase? This course has helped me to discover Jesus as . . .

> If you have extra time, use the following additional questions.

2. What new insights have you gained by participating in this study?

3. What changes in your attitude and/or behavior will you carry with you?

4. Do you think this study will have any impact on your church? Explain.

Summary *(1 minute)*

> Participant's Guide page 102

Jesus really is beyond our full comprehension! He is so radically unlike anyone else who has ever lived. And the impact of his life continues today throughout the world.

This course has been designed to help us think about Jesus in new ways. Hopefully you've been challenged to discover a Jesus *you* never knew. Try to take at least one idea with you out into our world—and make a difference for him.

Planning Notes

LOOK AT PG 101 ... PREFER (WE DISCUS
QUESTION #3 (*)

- SOLICIT PRAYERS

- TALK ABOUT WHAT'S NEXT (SUSAN)

- CLOSING PRAYER

Video Notes
Philip Yancey

This course has helped me to discover Jesus as . . .

- <u>Sure</u>: Bud Johnson — progression is hard to be positive
- <u>Ruth</u>: For Scott + family
- <u>Dave</u>: Fire Season, Commune in retirement, employment for Dave, State/Federal vocation rehab program approval, summary steps forward, finances

---

Summary

In this session we:

• Learned about and discussed the different facets of Jesus' life.

• Shared our own discoveries of who Jesus is.

Suggested Reading

For more thoughts on this session's topic, read
"The Difference He Makes,"
chapter 14 of *The Jesus I Never Knew*.

Appendix

Movie Credits

Cotton Patch Gospel—Scenes from this video appear courtesy of Bridgestone Multi Media Group, Chandler, AZ. To order a copy of the complete video program, call 1–800–523–0988 or send a check or money order for $19.95 + $3.00 S&H (AZ residents add 7% tax) to: Bridgestone Multi Media Group, 300 North McKemy Ave., Chandler, AZ 85226, ATT: Cotton Patch Gospel Order Dept.

The Gospel According to St. Matthew—Scenes from this video appear courtesy of The Cifex Corporation, Southampton, NY. Telephone: 1–516–283–4795

Cecil B. De Mille's King of Kings—Scenes from this video are by permission of Modern Sound Pictures, Inc./Gordon Films, Inc., New York, NY. Telephone: 1–212–757–9390

Heaven—Footage from Diane Keaton's *Heaven* appears courtesy of Lightyear Entertainment, New York, NY. Telephone: 1–212–563–4610

Jesus—Scenes from this video are extracted from the *New Media Bible* as published by the Genesis Project, N. V.

Jesus of Nazareth—Footage from this video appears courtesy of Polygram Television, Beverly Hills, CA. Telephone: 1–310–724–8100

Witnesses—Written and performed by Curt Cloninger. Produced and distributed by Gospel Films, Inc., PO Box 455, Muskegon, MI 49443 Telephone: 1–800–253–0413

Son of Man—Film clips appear courtesy of the estate of Dennis Potter/BBC Worldwide Americas, Inc.

Gospel Road—Film clips courtesy of Johnny Cash

Additional Films to Use as Resources

Having seen some of the film clips, you may decide you want to view one or more of the films in their entirety. At times it may be difficult to locate a film, but most are available through your local Christian bookstore or film distributor, or can be obtained from a video rental store such as Blockbuster.

However, keep in mind that there are daunting copyright issues for those who show the movies to an organized group in a church building. (Showing movies in a home, with no admissions charge, is okay.) The film clip segments provided in the curriculum have all been approved and permission received for this specific project. For viewing other films the Motion Picture Licensing

Corporation offers a renewable overall license for $95 per congregation, allowing you to show portions of movies at one location only for a year. Showing a video without the copyright owner's authorization is a copyright infringement and risks fines ranging from $500 to $20,000. For more details or to receive a license application, write the Motion Picture Licensing Corporation at P.O. Box 66970, Los Angeles, CA 90066 or call 1–800–462–8855 or 1–310–822–8855.

If you can overcome these hurdles, you may find that viewing additional films adds a lot to your study of Jesus. Listed below are some of the movies Philip Yancey used with his class in Chicago, along with his personal evaluation. These films will give you a great deal to think about!

Movie Appendix

Where can you obtain the following videos? If they are still in current release, you can order most of them through a large video chain, such as Blockbuster. They usually have a catalog of "films in print." More obscure films can be found through an "art film" distributor, such as Facets Video in Chicago (1–800–331–6197). Explicitly Christian films may be ordered at your local Christian bookstore or obtained through a distributor such as Gospel Films (call 1–800–253–0413 or contact them at http://www.gospelcom.net/gf/ on the Internet). Gateway Films is another outlet (1–800–523–0226). Several Catholic distributors have good supplies of videos as well, so you may want to contact a Catholic school or library for leads. (Try Ignatius Press at 1–800–651–1531.)

These are some of the movies I showed my class, listed in order of their potential usefulness to you.

The Visual Bible: It is a new, lavish production, very faithful to biblical texts. The Gospel of Matthew has been released in three volumes. The owners of this film may be willing to accommodate requests for more lenient copyright restrictions. Write Gener8Xion Entertainment, Inc., P.O. Box 6548–347, Orange, CA 92613 or call 1–800–332–4253.

The Greatest Story Ever Told: In an incredible miscasting, this movie features Max von Sydow in the lead role, so Jesus speaks with a thick Scandinavian accent. The other characters in the film act like zombies, giving no reactions. Nevertheless, the cinematography is beautiful (the setting looks to me more like Utah than Israel), and there are some fine scenes. Stocked in many video chains.

King of Kings II: Samuel Bronston remade DeMille's classic some thirty years later. Widely available, this movie stays mostly faithful to the gospel narratives, at least as seen through the eyes of Hollywood screenwriters.

The Last Temptation of Christ: Perhaps I should not even mention this film, since its release sparked furious controversy and a nationwide boycott. Some churches may find it so offensive as to have nothing to do with it. Indeed, the movie contains objectionable scenes as well as speculative and perhaps heretical theology (especially in the last forty minutes of the film). Yet I must admit that individual scenes scattered here and there throughout the film have great power. Taken as a whole, the film is a bore, hardly deserving the intense reactions it aroused. Taken in pieces, it offers much food for thought. It is available for rental in local video stores, and a wise leader can, with discretion, incorporate some scenes into a group discussion. Everything depends on the group. If some members are easily offended or have a visceral reaction against the very idea of using this movie, don't force it. Note that Paul Schroeder, who wrote the screenplay, attended Calvin College, although he later abandoned much of his faith.

Godspell: To my knowledge, this movie is no longer available for sale, although sometimes it is shown on HBO or other pay channels. If a group member notices a showing (movies about Jesus usually get airplay around Christmas and Easter), the group may want to devote an entire meeting to watching it together. It's funky, overwrought, and dated, showing the excesses of the sixties at their worst. At the time of release, however, it helped change the consciousness of many people, giving them a new vision of Jesus as a clown dressed up in a Superman outfit. Despite the weird settings, the musical's texts tend to stay faithful to the Gospels.

Jesus of Montreal: Must be used with discretion, as it contains some nudity and clearly unorthodox theology. Yet the movie is one of the most creative attempts in recent years to bring Jesus into a modern context. An acting troupe in Montreal takes on the task of presenting the Passion play in new forms, and in the process the actor playing Jesus becomes obsessed, even delusional, acting out new variations on scenes from Jesus' life. Provocative and powerful when viewed as a whole, the movie would probably work best in individual scenes when used in a group, since some of the content might be offensive. Can be purchased or rented through the major video chains.

Jesus Christ, Superstar: Hollywood made an arty version of the Broadway musical. It's all spectacle and fluff, and I never found much usable material in it, but it does present some arty scenes with a strong musical background.

Others: Don't limit yourself to full-length movies about Jesus. You can easily adapt individual scenes from, say, *Oh, God!* starring George Burns and John Denver, or from the more recent *Dear God* or from the TV show *Touched by an Angel* or from the rash of movies about angels. Use your creativity. If one of your favorite movies includes a scene of supernatural mystery or of prayer or portrays a Christian in a certain light, it may well prompt a good discussion on the topic.

If you want further background on the movies, a book titled *Divine Images: A History of Jesus on the Screen* by Roy Kinnard and Tim Davis, gives extensive coverage of just about every movie ever made about Jesus.

About the Writer

Sheryl Moon is a consultant for various churches and organizations and a freelance writer. Her projects have ranged from designing a Christian education elective program for high school youth to writing guidebooks for video curriculum, including the *Saving Your Marriage Before It Starts* curriculum by Drs. Les and Leslie Parrott. Sheryl lives in Grand Rapids, Michigan, with her husband and son.

> ## "There is nothing we can do to make God love us more. There is nothing we can do to make God love us less."

We speak often of grace. But do we understand it? More important, do we truly *believe* in it . . . and do our lives proclaim it as powerfully as our words?

Grace is the church's great distinctive. It's the one thing the world cannot duplicate, and the one thing it craves above all else—for only grace can bring hope and transformation to a jaded world.

In this book, Yancey explores grace at street level. If grace is God's love for the undeserving, he asks, then what does it look like in action? And if Christians are its sole dispensers, then how are we doing at lavishing grace on a world that knows far more of cruelty and unforgiveness than it does of mercy?

Grace does not excuse sin, says Yancey, but it treasures the sinner. True grace is shocking, scandalous. It shakes our conventions with its insistence on getting close to sinners and touching them with mercy and hope.

In his most personal and provocative book ever, Yancey offers compelling, true portraits of grace's life-changing power. He searches for its presence in his own life and in the church. He asks, How can Christians contend graciously with moral issues that threaten all they hold dear?

And he challenges us to become living answers to a world that desperately wants to know, *What's So Amazing About Grace?*

Hardcover 0-310-21327-4
Audio Pages® Abridged Cassettes 0-310-21578-1
Audio Pages® Unabridged Cassettes 0-310-23228-7
Study Guide 0-310-21904-3

Pick up your copy of *What's So Amazing About Grace?*
at Christian bookstores near you.

ZONDERVAN

GRAND RAPIDS, MICHIGAN 49530 U!

WWW.ZONDERVAN.COM

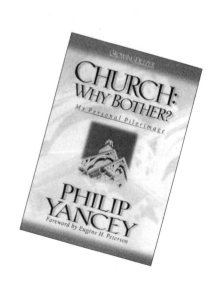

The Gift of Pain

The autobiography of Dr. Paul Brand follows his dramatic career in medicine across three continents.

Softcover 0-310-22144-7

Fearfully and Wonderfully Made

Philip Yancey teams with Dr. Paul Brand to offer insight into the marvelous details of the human body and draw analogies to the relationship expressed by New Testament writers in the metaphor of the body of Christ.

Softcover 0-310-35451-X

In His Image

The companion to *Fearfully and Wonderfully Made* unfolds spiritual truths through a physician's knowledge of the blood, the head, the spirit, and pain.

Softcover 0-310-35501-X

ZONDERVAN

GRAND RAPIDS, MICHIGAN 49530 US

WWW.ZONDERVAN.COM

We want to hear from you. Please send your comments about this
book to us in care of the address below. Thank you.

GRAND RAPIDS, MICHIGAN 49530 USA

WWW.ZONDERVAN.COM